Ten Questions
Every Pastor Fears*

*Answers Included

Ten Questions Every Pastor Fears*

*Answers Included

F. Belton Joyner Jr.

Abingdon Press
Nashville

TEN QUESTIONS EVERY PASTOR FEARS

This book is printed on acid-free paper.

Library of Congress Cataloging-in-Publication Data

Joyner, F. Belton.
    Ten questions every pastor fears / F. Belton Joyner, Jr.
        p.   cm.
    ISBN 978-0-687-65590-8 (pbk. : alk. paper)
    1. Pastoral theology.   2. Theology, Doctrinal—Miscellanea.   I. Title.

    BV4013.J69 2009
    233—dc22

                                                                    2008034476

Scripture quotations unless otherwise noted are from the New Revised Standard Version Bible, copyright ©1989, by the Division of Christian Education of the National Council of the Churches of Christ in the U.S.A. Used by permission. All rights reserved.

The scripture quotation noted KJV is from the King James Version.

09 10 11 12 13 14 15 16 17 18—10 9 8 7 6 5 4 3 2 1

MANUFACTURED IN THE UNITED STATES OF AMERICA

For
Diane M. Christianson
and
W. Bryan Faggart

My pastors who have handled my feared questions

CONTENTS

CONTENTS

OPENING MUMBLING:

AN INTRODUCTION

T hese beginning pages are called "mumbling" because
often that is the best we can do when confronted
with a feared question. Perhaps we burble until we
can get our thoughts organized. Perhaps we murmur because we have no idea what to say. Perhaps we mutter because we have asked ourselves the same feared question
that has now been posed to us.

Mumbling might even be a spiritual discipline. Instead of
loudly proclaiming with faked absolute assurance something that actually remains quite ungelled in one's own
heart, one mumbles. There is a certain authenticity about
mumbling: a little of this and a little of that and maybe
some of the other. Although the penetrating words of Revelation 3:16 can be haunting ("So, because you are lukewarm, and neither cold nor hot, I am about to spit you out
of my mouth"), there is comfort in Paul's advice to Titus:
"But as for you, teach what is consistent with sound doctrine" (Titus 2:1). So, I can say to myself, "I am mumbling
not because I am lukewarm; I am mumbling because I am
sorting out sound doctrine!"

Of course, some of our colleagues—perhaps including
you—do not fear the difficult questions. The spiritual and

intellectual challenge excites such a person. They have long since ceased being "tossed to and fro and blown about by every wind of doctrine" (Ephesians 4:14a) and have a solid grasp on the truth that they now speak in love (Ephesians 4:15a). I am grateful for them and pray for their patience as some of the rest of us struggle to hear more clearly what God is saying.

Why are some questions "feared questions"? Pastors recognize that they are the intentional theologians of a congregation. If anyone is expected to have sorted through the tricky places of theological and biblical wonderment, it is the pastor. What if I fail as a theologian—does that mean I fail as a pastor? None of us wants to look ignorant or sloppy in spiritual matters. The pressure is on! Handling the subtle places of doubt and belief is no small task. No wonder some questions are dreaded.

ABOUT THIS BOOK

This book is one pastor's thinking about issues that often emerge in the ordinary flow of pastoral work. There is an arrogance in writing this book. Not only is there a dangerous presumption that I have spotted ten questions that are stirring in every congregation, I have dared to offer answers. I trust that you understand that my "mumblings" are an invitation to conversation, both with the book and with the questions addressed.

The Feared Question

The first part of each chapter is a presentation of a feared question. Part of the nature of such inquiries is that they show up when we least expect them: in the parking lot, at a ball game, at a precinct voting station. In these settings, pastors are not always equipped with their full theological armor and certainly do not have with them notes from Systematic Theology 101. Biblical resources will probably be what one can carry in head and heart. Although "Let me get back to you on that" might buy a little time, the power of the question lingers.

Most pastors can identify with these dismaying moments. The eyes of the congregation's matriarch aim a steady bead on the pastor as she walks purposefully across the room. Uh-oh! The major giver to the building fund sits with arms crossed in a defiant mode as the church council discusses missions. Uh-oh! The youth who is just back from a mountaintop experience at camp comes up with tears in his eyes. Uh-oh! The thorn-in-the-flesh nonbeliever spots the pastor on the street the day after a damaging hurricane. Uh-oh! The six-year-old child is mad at God because her parents have divorced. Uh-oh!

Dreaded questions can show up in study groups, but their very nature of catching us with our best thinking antenna down means that they often show up unexpectedly. I hope you enjoy the thrill of roller-coaster theology because these questions are bound to come.

Quick, First Thoughts

Before we begin giving a serious answer to a question, we often have flash notions that are best kept to ourselves. The second part of each chapter is a brief hunch on what those instant reactions might be. Fortunately, most of us have filters in place that will keep us from saying these things out loud! Spiritual dialogue is not promoted (usually!) by our exasperatingly saying to the questioner: "And what made you think that I can give a happy hoot about your question until I have finished my dessert?" "Quick, First Thoughts" allow us to own our feelings without giving up our control over them.

Thinking a Bit More about It

The major portion of each chapter is a tracing of biblical and theological and pastoral matters that emerge in reflecting on the question. Although classic religious studies language is not always used, there are major theological points in each encounter.

Question 1 ("Is my Jewish neighbor going to hell?") touches on soteriology, eschatology, and the nature of God. What is the meaning of salvation?

Question 2 ("Why did God let my kitten die?") walks around in the great puddle of theodicy. If God is good and all-powerful, why do bad things happen?

Question 3 ("What do you mean, you changed the light that Grandma gave the church?") explores tradition and the nature of revelation. If God is a living God, does God change?

Question 4 ("Why doesn't your wife sing in the choir?") opens up concerns related to the pastoral office, the meaning of marriage, and discipleship. Does God call people to the pastorate one at a time or two at a time?

Question 5 ("Who are you going to vote for, Reverend?") looks at public policy, church-state relations, and ecclesiology. How is a pastor to be a good citizen?

Question 6 ("Why are you leaving us for another church? Don't you like us?") offers a chance to consider connectionalism, congregationalism, and the meaning of the Body of Christ. What is the best use of pastoral personnel?

Question 7 ("Why do you pick hymns that no one likes?") takes note of liturgics and hymnody. What priorities shape our worship experiences?

Question 8 ("Why do we keep sending money off for missions?") is a journeying around missions, ecclesiology, and financial stewardship. How do dollars define our values?

Question 9 ("Why can't we use Christmas red on the altar table during December?") travels around liturgics, the gospel, and ecclesiology. How does color reflect who we are?

Question 10 ("Are all acts of God acts of God?") unwraps subjects of theodicy, the nature of God, and the human condition. Who is responsible for bad things?

Throughout each chapter, I have tried to draw on relevant biblical sources. The temptation, of course, is to pick and choose among proof texts. I have endeavored to avoid that pull; and even when the quoted text does not extend to surrounding verses, I have made an effort to be faithful to context. (Of course, if you want to check me out, you will have to look up all the references and that won't be bad!)

The Bible carries the central theme of God's unfolding journey with God's people. The Scriptures represent God's self-revelation. In order to receive the full gift of that revelation, we have to consider individual passages in light of their place within the whole Bible. Passage A might appear to contradict Passage B. A living God among a living people is going to make an emphasis that is distinctive to the living moment. What is being said in Passage A? What is being said in Passage B? And what was going on that led God to inspire those words? John Wesley said that Scripture was twice inspired: once when written and once when read.

The theological expressions in "Thinking a Bit More about It" are, by necessity, cursory. Massive volumes have been written on all these themes. In this brief volume, the best we can do is shape some of the matters that must be considered. You can always scribble your notes—agreements, disagreements, questions—in the margins. (If you make those kinds of notes, when you accidentally leave the book in a chair at a regional pastors' meeting, the one who finds the volume will be quite impressed with your thoroughness.)

Occasionally, the thoughts in a chapter may seem more like the aforementioned mumbling than they do distinctive gospel proclamation. In a sense, pondering more than one side of a question is a way of honoring the question. To be open to more than one possible answer is to celebrate the astonishing mystery of God. To taste more than one flavor in responding is to respect the complexity of what is asked simply. And, truth to tell, sometimes I am still brooding over what God seems to be saying (or not saying).

Something to Say

After chasing the implications of each question, I have offered a short start to an answer. Keep in mind that the person who raised the "feared question" is still standing there, not having the benefit of the pages of reflection, and waiting for some kind of reply. If the "Thinking a Bit More about It" seems abbreviated, just consider how abrupt these little "Something to Say" answers will be! These brief replies are not so much summaries of the "heavy stuff" as they are beginnings to a conversation.

For that reason, each "Something to Say" usually ends with a question or some way of inviting dialogue. The questioner should be respected as a person who wonders but also as one who has something to offer to the pastor's own growth. Sometimes at a feeling level, sometimes at a thinking level, sometimes at an open-ended level, one's responses to "feared questions" should be a summons to keep the exchange going.

Let's Keep on Talking

Good questions often give birth to new questions. By including "Let's Keep on Talking" in each chapter, I have wanted to indicate that I recognize that my answers do not answer everything. There is more to be thought about! The best answers are those that tickle the imagination, that open doors rather than closing doors.

You, the reader, may want to chew on these additional questions on your own. You might get a Sunday school class or study group to engage them with you. You might try writing out your own answers to the questions.

The church certainly has answers, truth that grows out of exposure to Jesus Christ. We should not shirk from the saving revelation of God. We should not minimize the radical nature of God's grace. We should not pretend that God is without judgment. We should not let go of the promised hope of eternal life. But, having said all that, we should recognize that the church also needs to reflect the Master who himself raised questions, who added to what "you have heard of old," and who shared in the mystery of the godhead. To keep on asking questions is one way to live the truth.

Prayer

Each chapter ends with a prayer. Perhaps after struggling with difficult issues we are more aware than ever of our dependency upon divine power. The best we can offer is a frail imitation—even a shattered imitation—of the One in whose image we have been created. The remarkable reality about the God shown in Jesus Christ is that our weaknesses become building blocks for new strength, our repentance becomes the receptor for forgiveness, and our doubts become encountering places for the holy. No wonder we pray!

WAYS TO USE THIS BOOK

Although written primarily for pastors, this little book also could be a resource for a class or small group. To use the book in such a setting, one might begin by reading aloud the "Feared Question" section. Ask each participant to turn to a partner and talk about the answer he or she might give. Go through "Thinking a Bit More about It" and share some of the biblical references. Then have the partners exchange any new ideas with each other. Next, you could add your own theological insights (perhaps bouncing off those in the book). Finally, have each partner pair write a brief—fifty-word?—answer that might be given to the feared question. Invite teams to share their answers. Ask: "What new questions emerge from these answers?" Those fresh inquiries might be fodder for another class session. (If none are forthcoming, you could raise the "Let's Keep on Talking" questions.) Close with prayer, one from the book or one led by you or another class member.

?
QUESTION ONE

"IS MY JEWISH NEIGHBOR GOING TO HELL?"

THE FEARED QUESTION

Karla Carpenter seemed to be lingering after the final service of a preaching series at St. Mark Church. Pastor Clarence had heard the usual comments at the door ("Great sermon," "Thanks for that message," "I enjoyed that," "Did you really like my stewed apricots at the supper tonight?"), but he noticed that Ms. Carpenter seemed to be staying more for a conversation than for a quick word.

She began slowly. "I listened to what you said in the sermon. You said that Jesus was the way to salvation. I've got this neighbor, Mr. Baum. And he is"—she hesitated for a nanosecond before continuing—"a Jew. Now, Mr. Baum is a great neighbor, a fine man, a good citizen. But based on what you said in your sermon, I have this question: *Is my Jewish neighbor going to hell?*"

QUICK, FIRST THOUGHTS

Why do people insist on paying attention when I am preaching! I must have sounded as if I was drawing a spiritual line in the sand when I talked about Jesus as Savior. I can tell that Karen likes Mr. Baum and wants the best for him. I guess I should have seen this question coming. (And so that yellowish-orange stuff at supper tonight turned out to be stewed apricots.)

THINKING A BIT MORE ABOUT IT

How widely opened are the saving arms of God? Or, more to the point, does God ever sadly say, "No"?

Jesus himself seems to draw a rather clear line about how one can have access to God. He said, "No one comes to the Father except through me" (John 14:6). Later, Peter is speaking to the leaders of the Jewish community and says, "There is salvation in no one else, for there is no other name under heaven given among mortals by which we must be saved" (Acts 4:12).

Is it possible for someone to relate to God through Jesus Christ without that person's knowing the name of Jesus? Is the presence and power of Jesus Christ limited to those who recognize that power and presence as Jesus?

In biblical terms, "name" means the character, values, and quality of a person. A change of name suggests a change of character. (Thus, Saul's name is changed to Paul when he has the Damascus Road life-changing experience—Acts 13:9.) Does that imply that to be saved by the name of Jesus Christ is to be saved by the character, values, and quality of Jesus (seen in his death and resurrection)? Is it necessary to name the name?

Does Jesus claim as his own some whom others might consider outside the fold? In one account, Jesus describes himself as "the good shepherd [who] lays down his life for the sheep" (John 10:11). Who are these sheep for whom the Shepherd will die? Are Jews on that list? Are Gentiles on that list? Are nonbelievers on that list? Is Karla Carpenter's neighbor on that list?

Just as those listening to Jesus begin to make up their list of those for whom the good shepherd will die, our Lord says, in effect, "Whoa now! How are you so sure that your list is the same as my list? 'I have other sheep that do not belong to this fold. I must bring them also, and they will listen to my voice. So there will be one flock, one shepherd'" (John 10:16). The Master is saying, "The boundaries for my flock are more expansive than you think!"

The apostle Paul must have pondered this point. For example, in Romans 3:22, the Apostle speaks of "the righteousness of God through faith in Jesus Christ for all who believe." That seems like a fairly clear boundary: all who believe. On the other hand, in Romans 11:32, Paul writes, "For God has imprisoned all in disobedience so that he may be merciful to all." That seems like a fully open door: all.

Which of those views represents God's clearest revelation?

One way the church has sought to answer that question is in the historic creeds. The Apostles' Creed, formulated between the fourth and seventh centuries, makes the claim that Jesus "descended into hell." (Some versions say, "descended to the dead.") Why would the church make such a profession? Perhaps the reality is that no one, of any time or place, of any spiritual circumstance, of any brokenness or negation, is separated from the Messiah, the saving

11

Messiah. "For I am convinced that neither death, nor life, nor angels, nor rulers, nor things present, nor things to come, nor powers, nor height, nor depth, nor anything else in all creation, will be able to separate us from the love of God in Christ Jesus our Lord" (Romans 8:38-39).

If Jesus' death is for all—and he descended to the dead—then his resurrection is for all. The atonement is universal. The demonic has been defeated. Our Lord saw it coming. Early in his ministry, he sent out seventy to be about a practice of healing and a proclamation that God's reign was coming into the midst of the people (Luke 10:1-3). When these seventy returned with stories of how the demonic was defeated (Luke 10:17), Jesus announced the defeat of Satan: "I watched Satan fall from heaven like a flash of lightning" (Luke 10:18). Jesus wins. Satan loses.

Does Jesus give that victory to everyone or only to those who believe in him? The Scriptures say that "all Israel will be saved" (Romans 11:26). The scriptures say that "just as one man's trespass [Adam] led to condemnation for all, so one man's act of righteousness [Jesus Christ] leads to justification and life for all" (Romans 5:18). The scriptures say that "all people shall see the glory of the LORD together" (Isaiah 40:5b).

Does Jesus give that victory to everyone or only to those who believe in him? The Scriptures say, "Believe on the Lord Jesus, and you will be saved" (Acts 16:31). That was the answer of Paul and Silas to the jailer who asked how he might be saved. But the account goes on to indicate that the jailer's entire family was baptized. Did you ever wonder how the household was saved by the faith of the jailer alone? They were all baptized even though the text mentions only that the jailer was a believer (Acts 16:32-34).

Does Jesus give that victory to everyone or only to those who believe in him? The Scriptures say, "Everyone who believes in [God's only Son] may not perish but may have eternal life" (John 3:16b). The Scriptures say, "Everyone who believes that Jesus is the Christ has been born of God" (1 John 5:1). The Scriptures say, "Very truly, I tell you, anyone who hears my word and believes him who sent me has eternal life, and does not come under judgment, but has passed from death to life" (John 5:24).

It seems like such a simple question: *Does Jesus give that victory to everyone or only to those who believe in Him?* Most of us—myself included—probably come to that inquiry pretty sure what the answer might be. Oh, there are gray areas around the edges (What of babies who die? What of persons who are never presented an opportunity to accept Jesus Christ? Can a person gain and then lose salvation?), but the direct answer to the question seems obvious. Christians say clearly that one must believe in Jesus Christ to be made whole, to be saved, to go to heaven. After all, the same Apostles' Creed that declares that Jesus descended into hell (to the dead) also claims that "he shall come to judge the quick and the dead" (that is, the living and the dead). Where I come from, that about covers everybody (although I did hear someone say that "the quick and the dead" sounded like a description of the Los Angeles Freeway).

However. On the other hand. But. Nevertheless. Conversely. There are still biblical evidences of a God who gathers with grace more magnetic than we have imagined, grace powerful enough to draw all souls to God. "Indeed, God did not send the Son into the world to condemn the world, but in order that the world might be saved through him" (John 3:17).

In *Explanatory Notes Upon the New Testament*, John Wesley

13

explored how Peter addressed the question of who found favor with God. Acts 10:34-35 notes what Peter said: "Then Peter began to speak to them: 'I truly understand that God shows no partiality, but in every nation anyone who fears him and does what is right is acceptable to him.' "

Wesley comments (using his own translation):

> *But in every nation he that feareth him, and worketh righteousness*—He that first reverences God, as great, wise, good: the Cause, End, and Governor of all things; and, secondly, from this awful regard to Him, not only avoids all known evil, but endeavours, according to the best light he has, to do all things well. *Is accepted of him*— Through Christ, though he knows Him not. The assertion is express and admits of no exception. He is in the favour of God, whether enjoying His written word and ordinances or not. (John Wesley, *Explanatory Notes upon the New Testament* [Naperville, Ill.: Alec R. Allenson, 1958] 434-35)

Is Wesley right that it is sufficient for one to live "according to the best lights he has"? Is it, as Wesley suggests, possible to be accepted through Christ even though one does not know Christ?

The biblical witness speaks of a judgment against those who ignore the vulnerable: hungry, unclothed, imprisoned, lonely (Matthew 25:31-46). Matthew quotes Jesus as saying that the servant who does not do the master's work will be thrown "into the outer darkness" (Matthew 25:30). The psalmist reminds us that

> [the LORD] is coming to judge the earth.
> He will judge the world with righteousness,
>   and the peoples with his truth. (Psalm 96:13b, c)

John's vision was of a heavenly tribunal where persons were "judged according to their works" (Revelation 20:12).

There is a biblical theme of judgment. Is that judgment based on right action or right belief?

What is the good news in the midst of this rollercoaster of ideas? Jesus is clear that he came to save the world: "I do not judge anyone who hears my words and does not keep them, for I came not to judge the world, but to save the world" (John 12:47). Yet, Jesus is also clear that there is a judge of the one who rejects him: "The one who rejects me and does not receive my word has a judge; on the last day the word that I have spoken will serve as judge" (John 12:48).

The good news is that our lawyer is the judge! That's not a bad deal—not a bad deal for me, for you, for Karla Carpenter, or for Karla Carpenter's Jewish neighbor. "My little children, I am writing these things to you so that you may not sin. But if anyone does sin, we have an advocate with the Father, Jesus Christ the righteous; and he is the atoning sacrifice for our sins, and not for ours only but also for the sins of the whole world" (1 John 2:1-2).

Frederick Faber (1854) summarized this good news in this hymn poem:

> There's a wideness in God's mercy like the wideness of the sea; there's a kindness in God's justice, which is more than liberty.
>
> For the love of God is broader than the measure of our mind; and the heart of the Eternal is most wonderfully kind.
>
> If our love were but more simple, we should rest upon God's word; and our lives would be illumined by the presence of our Lord.

SOMETHING TO SAY

Karla, God bless you for your concern for your neighbor! There is certainly mystery about God and God's relationship with us. After all, God is more than we can fathom. But it is my belief and trust that Jesus Christ is the full revelation of God. What I see in Jesus is both an acceptance of all people and a call to faithful discipleship. Once when Jesus was teaching about the kingdom of God, he said the kingdom was not about our sorting who is evil and who is good, but to trust that judgment to the one who owns the field (Matthew 13:30). I am willing to do that, and in the meantime I testify to the goodness and love of the one revealed in Jesus Christ. Does that make sense?

LET'S KEEP ON TALKING

1. What about God's saving relationship with Muslims? With Buddhists? With atheists?

2. What is the meaning of my free will, my freedom of choice, if God just keeps on loving (saving) me regardless of my response?

3. What is the responsibility of Christians to proclaim what God has revealed in Jesus Christ?

PRAYER

God of gathering grace, grant me a humble spirit that accepts the fullness of your love, not just for me, but for all people. I confess that I stumble in trying to understand what it means that you are for all people when there are some who say no to you. Keep me close to your tender mercies. And use me as you would, as a witness to those who do not know the good news of Jesus Christ, in whose name I pray. Amen.

QUESTION TWO

"WHY DID GOD LET MY KITTEN DIE?"

THE FEARED QUESTION

Barbara McArthur was getting into her car, ready for a quick bite and the afternoon nap that usually followed the busy Sunday morning activities. There were only a couple of other vehicles in the parking lot of Merritt Memorial Church. "Rev. Barbara! Rev. Barbara!" The pastor stepped out of her car to answer the shout of her name. It was Buster Shuler. Next to him stood Francine, his five-year-old daughter.

"Francine wanted to ask you something," Mr. Shuler said. The Reverend Ms. McArthur turned and looked into the tear-stained eyes of the young child. Francine's voice trembled with hurt. "This morning when you had the children down at the front," she began, "you told us that God loved us and wanted the best for us and always took care of us."

"Yes, I did. Isn't that wonderful?" soothed the pastor.

"And you said that God loved and cared for our pets too."

"Indeed! And wants us to take care of them," Ms. McArthur added.

The tears welled up again in Francine's eyes: "Then, *why did God let my kitten die?*"

QUICK, FIRST THOUGHTS

I'm a sucker for a child who is crying. Why didn't I get out of the parking lot before Francine spotted me! She really loved that little cat. Now how can I explain all this in a way a five-year-old can understand? I'm thirty-seven years old and I'm not sure I understand! And I wonder if this is something that came up that day I cut out of my theology class in order to get to the ball game on time!

THINKING A BIT MORE ABOUT IT

The apostle Paul knew that suffering, loss, and death were part of the human condition. But he carried the thought a notch beyond that. "We know that the whole creation has been groaning in labor pains until now" (Romans 8:22). It is not just humankind that suffers from brokenness from God's intentional will; all of the created order (including cats!) suffers from that impairment. The whole creation groans for a new birth into life.

What about new life for all creatures? When Paul wrote the church at Colossae, he reminded them that the hope of the gospel was for all creation: "every creature under heaven" (Colossians 1:23c). When John stated what was revealed to him about God's full reign, he wrote, "And the one who was seated on the throne said, 'See, I am making all things new'" (Revelation 21:5). God promises a new creation because the old creation is broken. Dare we say that kittens die because the creation has fallen?

Think about the Genesis account of creation. When God confronts Adam about having eaten of the forbidden fruit (Genesis 3:11), the man is quick to pass the blame on to Eve (Genesis 3:12). When God confronts the woman about this disobedience, she is quick to pass the blame on to the serpent (Genesis 3:13). There seems to be enough blame to go around!

When God spells out the result of this fall from God's boundaries (the punishment for sin), God speaks to the serpent (Genesis 3:14), to the woman (Genesis 3:16), and to the man (Genesis 3:17). Humankind and serpent alike suffer the consequences of this first sin. The sin separated humankind from God but also brought the entire created order under judgment.

The ripple effect of sin is like a row of dominos falling onto one another, each one toppling the one next to it. For example, as soon as Adam and Eve break their relationship with God, they become broken from each other. Prior to their act of defiance, they live happily with one another, but as soon as they violate God's will, they become broken from each other too. Suddenly, they know they are naked, and in embarrassment (and as a sign of their separation from each other), they seek fig leaves to make loincloths (Genesis 3:7). Disconnection from God leads to disconnection from each other.

The same enmity that has come between the human beings has also come between humankind and the serpent (Genesis 3:15). What God has intended for good ("and God saw that it was good"—Genesis 1:10, 12, 18, 21, 25, 31) has turned into shattered goodness. God created humankind and the rest of creation to live in harmony, but the same disobedience that changed the way Adam and Eve related to God and to each other also changed the way that humanity and creation related. The writer of Genesis uses the term "enmity" (Genesis 3:15)—hostility, antagonism. Clearly, what was intended for life has fallen into the valley of the shadow of death.

An anonymous poet penned it this way:

> God's plan made a hopeful beginning,
> But we spoiled our chances by sinning.
> We trust that the story
> Will end in God's glory,
> But, at present, the other side's winning!

God created things to be in good relationship.

> For thus says the LORD,
> who created the heavens
>   (he is God!),
> who formed the earth and made it
>   (he established it;
> he did not create it a chaos,
>   he formed it to be inhabited!):
> I am the LORD and there is no other. (Isaiah 45:18)

So, why do little kittens die? Because all of creation is fallen.

Adam and Eve. It's all their fault. At least, I'd like to think that the Genesis story is about them "back then" and not about me "here and now." It's not that simple. The name "Adam" means "human being." The name "Eve" means "life giver." Do you begin to see how this is not only a story about a man and a woman who lived long ago? It is also told as the story of my life and your life. If it is an account

of "human being" and "life giver," it does not give me much
room for hiding. (Besides, hiding does not work too well
with God—Genesis 3:8.) Our kinship with the earth—the
rest of creation—begins to unfold when the storyteller
makes a point of saying the human is made of dirt!

All of this is to say that as inheritors of Adam and Eve, we
continue to live their story. It is also our story. Brokenness.
The fall of humankind and the fall of the created order are
part of one piece. Humankind is created in the image of
God (Genesis 1:27). It is that image that gets shattered in
the fall. Being in the image of God means humans are created for relationship with God, with one another, and with
the created order. So, the fall of humankind expresses itself
in a broken relationship with God, a broken relationship
with one another, and brokenness in the created order.

This brokenness means that all living things die, be they
carrots or be they Christians. When that death occurs is
shaped by many intertwined factors: personal health, outside influences, environmental impact, accidents, healing
touches, nourishment, and (for more complex forms of life)
emotional well-being. Where is God in all of this?

God does not will everything that God allows. In grant-
ing free will to the human creature, God has allowed us to
stumble, mumble, and crumble as we make our choices.
Jesus is the only one who made perfect use of free will. As
the writer of Philippians reminds us:

> Let the same mind be in you that was in Christ Jesus,
> who, though he was in the form of God,
>   did not regard equality with God
>   as something to be exploited,
> but emptied himself,
>   taking the form of a slave,
>   being born in human likeness.

And being found in human form,
he humbled himself
and became obedient to the point of death—
even death on a cross. (Philippians 2:5-8)

Trembling around the edges of this discussion is this question: *Do animals go to heaven?* (Will our deceased pets be in heaven?) For starters, we ought to acknowledge that our knowledge of heaven is revealed knowledge, not something we figured out by observation and experience. My context for reflecting on this issue is something my mother said to me when (around the age ten) I asked if it snowed in heaven. She replied, "It does if God thinks it is best for us." Heaven is put together in the way that God thinks is best for us. That's good enough for me.

We are not the first to wonder about what happens to animals after death. The writer of Ecclesiastes wrote, "For the fate of humans and the fate of animals is the same; as one dies, so dies the other. They all have the same breath, and humans have no advantage over the animals; for all is vanity. All go to one place; all are from the dust, and all turn to dust again. Who knows whether the human spirit goes upward and the spirit of animals goes downward to the earth?" (Ecclesiastes 3:19-21).

Some people ask the question as, "Do animals have souls?" Some people ask the question as, "Are animals included in the resurrection of the body?" Some people ask the question as, "Are you kidding?" Most Christian tradition teaches that the answer to all three questions is *no*. Only humankind is created in the image of God. Even though some animals seem to exude personality, they do not carry the gift of free will.

John Wesley is reported to have preached a sermon in

which he suggested that God's justice would give an after-life to animals because of their earthly suffering (Oxfordanimalethics.com). Are animals subject to God's judgment between the righteous and the unrighteous? All animals? Dogs? Horses? Pigs? Aardvarks? Two-toed sloths? Deer? Flounder? Robins? Vultures? Only domesticated animals? We are tempted to feel that it is more likely that our pets will meet us in heaven than it is that the grizzly bear we shot in the Alaskan wilderness will be there. But Jesus has said that relationships are different in heaven—"For in the resurrection they neither marry nor are given in marriage" (Matthew 22:30a)—so we might wonder if our relationships with animals will be the same in heaven as on earth. The truth is that our faith is to be in the power of God and not in earthly relationships.

God has given humankind responsibility for (dominion over—Genesis 1:26) all the animals. God has allowed humankind to name the animals (Genesis 2:20). There is a distinction between the one who names and the one who is named.

The gift of love with our animal companions is one of the richest marks of God's grace in our lives. The God who has granted us such a blessing surely cares enough to share in our sorrow when the broken nature of creation tears into such love.

SOMETHING TO SAY

Francine, I am really sorry that your kitten has died. You must have loved her very much, and I'm sure your kitten was glad to have you for a friend. God is sad when one of God's creatures dies, so God is sad along with you. The way the world works now is that living things do die. But guess what—God is not through with this world yet, so some day God's victory over death will be for all. Francine, tell me about your kitten.

LET'S KEEP ON TALKING

1. Why does God allow things to happen that are not God's intentional will?

2. What is the difference between wild animals and domesticated animals?

3. What is the difference between our eating meat and cannibalism?

PRAYER

Creator God, because we have desired to be in charge of your universe, we have messed up things. You have made us for healthy relationships, but we have broken your gift of creation. The energy of death seems to overwhelm us, but we look once more to the resurrected Savior and make claim upon a tomorrow that lives as a new earth and a new heaven, when all things will be created anew, through Jesus Christ our Lord. Amen.

?

QUESTION THREE

"WHAT DO YOU MEAN, YOU CHANGED THE LIGHT THAT GRANDMA GAVE THE CHURCH?"

THE FEARED QUESTION

Things had gone very smoothly at the church council meeting. The plans for the men's retreat were accepted. The special gift for hunger relief was approved. The trustees' report on new lighting for the narthex was received. The discussion about how the congregation might deal with neighborhood gang violence was civil. The recommendation to hire a part-time secretary passed. Pastor Garcia breathed a sigh of relief and thought to himself, *We avoided a number of bumps in the road tonight!*

Before the pastor could gather up his papers, Esther Perkins was standing squarely in front of him. "My family has been members of this church since 1904. My great-grandfather gave the land for this building. My grandmother paid the pastor's salary when the church almost went broke during the depression. My mother was volunteer choir director for twenty-six years. And I don't think I need to tell you what my husband and I do at this church these days."

Mr. Garcia took a deep breath and said, "Ah, Esther, I think something must be bothering you."

"*Bothering me* is a pretty mild way to put it. I heard that trustees' report about changing the lighting in the narthex. *What do you mean, you changed the light Grandma gave the church?"*

QUICK, FIRST THOUGHTS

Stay calm. Keep cool. Don't let her get your goat. But who in the world would have thought we needed to get her permission to change the lights in that narthex? It was as dark as the inside of a whale and we had to do something.

THINKING A BIT MORE ABOUT IT

The Bible has 149 words that can be translated *new*. Forms of the word *change* show up 81 times. The biblical journey is nothing if it is not about change, conversion, new beginnings, unexpected directions, and altered paths. God is in the "making new" business. Redemption.

Someone has noted that saints have a past and sinners have a future. That speaks of change!

The psalmist celebrates how God has "put a new song in my mouth" (Psalm 40:3a).

The prophet Isaiah hears God promise a different future:

I am about to do a new thing;
   now it springs forth, do you not perceive it?
                (Isaiah 43:19ab)

How does Jeremiah understand God's pledge to God's people? "The days are surely coming, says the LORD, when I will make a new covenant with the house of Israel and the house of Judah" (Jeremiah 31:31).

Ezekiel captures God's intent for God's faithful: "A new heart I will give you, and a new spirit I will put within you" (Ezekiel 36:26).

Jesus described his call to discipleship "a new commandment" (John 13:34).

Paul writes that there is new life in the Spirit (Romans 7:6).

Our Lord speaks of the Eucharistic cup as "the new covenant in my blood" (1 Corinthians 11:25b).

How does the apostle Paul depict life in Christ? "So if anyone is in Christ, there is a new creation: everything old has passed away; see, everything has become new!" (2 Corinthians 5:17).

John's vision of God's ultimate reign is called "a new heaven and a new earth" (Revelation 21:1) and declares that it is God who says, "See, I am making all things new" (Revelation 21:5).

In light of the evidence of this biblical sweep for newness, why is there resistance to change within the household of faith? Does opposition to change in physical surroundings mirror reluctance to change in spiritual climate? Sometimes, new wine means new wineskins (Mark 2:22). So, what's the big deal with Grandma's light?

Often, when persons oppose change, it is not the fear of change that bothers them; it is the fear of loss. Think of it like this: if the past has shaped me into who I am, then if I let go of the past, I have let go of part of who I am. That can be frightening. If I lose those symbols (light fixtures?) that connect me to the past, then I have perhaps lost the gifts of the past. That can be unnerving. If knowledge is power, then knowing the ways of the past gives me power in the present. That can be a heady experience.

The teacher in Ecclesiastes offers a caution about dwelling in the past:

> Do not say, "Why were the former days better than these?"
>   For it is not from wisdom that you ask this.
>
> (Ecclesiastes 7:10)

Jesus updated the moral code: "You have heard that it was said...But I say to you..." (Matthew 5:27-28). Our Lord said, "Again, you have heard that it was said to those of ancient times...But I say to you..." (Matthew 5:33-34). Was Jesus changing the light bulbs?

This newness is troublesome. In the old order, I know my place; I know where I fit in. And place is important! What is my role in the new order? God's people often seek the comfort of knowing what to expect. Did not the Israelites, even as they were escaping the harsh slavery of Egypt, complain that the old ways might have been better? "The whole congregation of the Israelites complained against Moses and Aaron in the wilderness. The Israelites said to them, 'If only we had died by the hand of the LORD in the land of Egypt, when we sat by the fleshpots and ate our fill of bread; for you have brought us out into this wilderness to kill this whole assembly with hunger'" (Exodus 16:2-3).

Longing for the past and seeking the comfortable assurance of the way things have been are not the only ingredients in resistance to change. There is also a pull to feel that longevity gives proprietorship. Church members often joke about persons who feel ownership of a pew "where our family has sat for fifty years." (The United Methodist Church, for example, has included in its *Discipline* a statement "that pews in The United Methodist Church shall always be free" [para. 2532, *The Book of Discipline of The United Methodist Church 2004* [Nashville: The United Methodist Publishing House, 2004], 489.) One reason new congregations tend to grow more rapidly than long-time congregations is the difficulty newcomers have of finding a place in the existing structures and institutional expressions of established churches.

It is not a sin to have a passionate interest in a faith community in which one has made a major life investment! It is, however, one thing to have a passionate interest and it is quite another thing to assume veto power over the community's ongoing life. At one point in the story of Israel, the Hebrew children began to feel their importance as a chosen people. They began to feel God chose them because they were so powerful and valuable. God corrected this misunderstanding: "It was not because you were more numerous than any other people that the LORD set his heart on you and chose you —for you were the fewest of all peoples. It was because the LORD loved you and kept the oath that he swore to your ancestors, that the LORD has brought you out with a mighty hand, and redeemed you from the house of slavery, from the hand of Pharaoh king of Egypt" (Deuteronomy 7:7-8). Note who the actor is in this summary: God set his heart; God chose you; God loved you; God kept the oath; God brought you out; God redeemed you. There is not much wiggle room for self-importance in that account!

The family of faith gives honor to those with longevity. Abraham and Sarah were advanced in years when God promised them a child, the beginning of a great nation (Genesis 18:10-11). The early church chose "elders" to be their leaders (Acts 14:23). John's vision of heavenly worship includes twenty-four elders who wear the crowns of victory (Revelation 4:4). The problem is not with longevity or tradition or heritage. The problem is with the presumption that authority and control go with "having been here since Adam." The biblical model is that authority is given, not grabbed or assumed.

When Jesus was unfolding his teaching ministry, the scribes and chief priests and leaders of the temple had a core question: *Who is it who gave you this authority?* (The question is important enough that all three synoptic accounts include it: Matthew 21:23, Mark 11:28, Luke 20:2.) Knowing the source of authority has a great deal to do with one's respect for that authority. In this chapter's "feared question," by what authority does Esther Perkins demand to know about the new lighting?

For most congregations, the largest space in their facilities is the space for worship. Often the most precious memorial gifts are present in the worship space: a cross given in memory of Aunt Susie, a pew to recognize Papa Joe, a stained glass window to honor three generations of family members, a hymnbook to remember a former pastor, kneelers presented in remembrance of someone's grandmother—the list goes on. To tamper with what happens in worship space is to tamper with quick-trigger emotions and feelings and memories.

Congregations that have become accustomed to a simple space for worship, an area often devoid of common Christian symbols, sometimes find themselves resisting the addition of accoutrements and accessories for worship. If, on the one hand, some congregations do not want to give up the "trappings" of their gathering space, others, on the other hand, do not want to add anything to theirs. What these congregations have in common is "Leave my worship space alone." Translation: Leave my worship alone. Translation: Leave my faith alone.

Is it wrong to hold on to tradition? Hardly! Jesus honored tradition when "he went to the synagogue on the sabbath day, as was his custom" (Luke 4:16b). Jesus honored tradition when he taught that "the kingdom of heaven is like the master of a household who brings out of his treasure [both] what is new and what is old" (Matthew 13:52). Jesus honored tradition when he identified himself as the one Isaiah told about:

> "I am the voice of one crying out in the wilderness,
> 'Make straight the way of the Lord.'" (John 1:23)

One of the Old Testament's most telling passages about tradition is revealed as Moses spoke to the people of Israel:

> When your children ask you in time to come, "What is the meaning of the decrees and the statutes and the ordinances that the LORD our God has commanded you?" then you shall say to your children, "We were Pharaoh's

slaves in Egypt, but the LORD brought us out of Egypt with a mighty hand. The LORD displayed before our eyes great and awesome signs and wonders against Egypt, against Pharaoh and all his household. He brought us out from there in order to bring us in, to give us the land that he promised on oath to our ancestors. Then the LORD commanded us to observe all these statutes, to fear the LORD our God, for our lasting good, so as to keep us alive, as is now the case. If we diligently observe this entire commandment before the LORD our God, as he has commanded us, we will be in the right." (Deuteronomy 6:20-25)

This text was written six hundred years after the Exodus, but the writer still refers to *we* being in Egypt, *we* being delivered from slavery. That old story is *our* story! And that heritage is honored by continuing to keep the commandments of God. As others have said: "Tradition is the living faith of dead believers; traditionalism is the dead faith of living believers."

Jesus had some harsh words to say to those who confused God's will with their own self-declared purposes: "You abandon the commandment of God and hold to human tradition" (Mark 7:8). Traditions that bring God's commandments into the present tense are good traditions. Traditions that prevent God's purposes from being realized in our time are bad traditions.

SOMETHING TO SAY

Esther, you and your family have been an important part of the life of this congregation. When we have been at our best as a church, often it has been because you have been at your best. The decision to change the lights in the narthex has been made in order to provide the most welcoming and hospitable entry we can provide for our building. I bet that is just why your grandmother gave that light in the first place!

LET'S KEEP ON TALKING

1. How do we keep tradition from becoming a barrier to mission instead of being a foundation upon which to stand?

2. How do we hold one another accountable for our motives in our life together as church?

3. What is the difference between change that is good and change that is harmful?

PRAYER

Merciful God, whose love has preceded us to our time and whose grace calls us to a new tomorrow, we thank you for the bounty you have poured upon our journey. We are grateful for those who came before us, those whose witness has been so strong that it still echoes in our lives. Grant us to hold hands with the past as we hold hands with the future you would give us, so that we may walk into newness of life, through Jesus Christ our Lord. Amen.

?

QUESTION FOUR

"WHY DOESN'T YOUR WIFE SING IN THE CHOIR?"

THE FEARED QUESTION

We want to celebrate the first anniversary of Mr. Gilmore as our pastor." Applause rippled through the fellowship hall of Langdoc Community Church.

"This has been a good year, I think we'll all agree. In fact, this has been a highlight year for Langdoc Church." A few "Amens" were added to the vigorous hand clapping.

"So this luncheon today is our way of saying thanks to our much loved, much appreciated, and much welcomed pastor, Andy Gilmore." Everyone in the room stood and added enthusiastic approval to the speech.

For Andy Gilmore, of course, it was an affirmation of the ministry he had brought to this struggling congregation. As someone had said, "This is the first time in a long time when Langdoc Community Church has talked more about tomorrow than about yesterday!" Andy Gilmore beamed.

As the well-wishers mingled and congratulated their pastor, Pat Russell stepped over and said, "Reverend, we are so glad to have you here at Langdoc! May I mention just one little thing that I think might help a bit? When Jennifer Calvin was our pastor, her husband, Clark, always sang in the choir. I know your wife has a beautiful voice. *Why doesn't your wife sing in the choir?*"

QUICK, FIRST THOUGHTS

Good grief! Why did Pat choose this moment to bring this up again! I thought I had made it clear that it is up to Yvonne to decide if she wants to sing in the choir. I wonder why Pat feels that she should mention this to me instead of directly inviting Yvonne.

THINKING A BIT MORE ABOUT IT

Instead of "Why doesn't your wife sing in the choir?" the inquiry might just as well be "Why doesn't your spouse teach Sunday school?" or "Why doesn't your husband go visiting with you?" or "Why doesn't your wife have the church council meeting at your house?" or "Why doesn't your husband direct the vacation Bible school...or go on the youth trip...or cook for the homeless shelter...or host the visiting missionary...or jump tall buildings in a single bound?"

Congregations looking toward a new pastor often secretly (or not so secretly) wish for a "two-fer." Will the spouse of the pastor play the piano, drive the church van, and fix coffee for the circle meeting? The spouse can be viewed as a second—unpaid—member of the pastoral team. Some congregations are disappointed to find out that the new pastor is single. If the single status works well for the pastor, why should the congregation feel cheated?

Truth to tell, there are some husbands and wives of pastors who cherish the myriad opportunities for work in a local church. They see it as their own ministry alongside the spouse. Singing in the choir and cleaning up after church suppers and teaching the "terrible twos" are occasions for a servant life to which they feel called.

This chapter is not about those husbands and wives. This chapter is not about those clergy spouses who understand themselves as co-worker with the pastor. This chapter is not about those who find fulfillment in the busy, busy life of "doing it all." This chapter is about those persons who do not appreciate the fact that a congregation has made expectations or assumptions about them and their involvement in the ebb and flow of the congregational time line. (My anecdotal evidence is that there are fewer and fewer congregations who make such demands. On the other hand, the anecdotal evidence is that spouses often feel guilty about their level of churchy involvement.)

Some couples have married before it was known that one of them would seek ordination or licensing as a pastor. In those cases, a dangerous question might be: "Would you have married me if you had known that I was going to be a pastor?"

There is some relevance to this circumstance in Matthew's account of the first Christmas when Joseph learns that Mary is pregnant. Should they call off their plans to marry? Should they go ahead and hope for the best?

Should they try to sort out all the implications of Mary's bearing a son for whom Joseph was not the biological father? Is it Mary's decision or is it Joseph's decision? Do either of them know what they are getting into? Luke tells us that Mary was mystified, but willing to deliver this child (Luke 1:38). Matthew tells us that Joseph was reassured that this unusual, unexpected pregnancy was part of God's plan (Matthew 1:20-21). They both went into this new relationship with an understanding of the terms of their marriage. If Mary asked Joseph, "Would you have married me if you knew that I was already pregnant?" Joseph could answer, "I knew!"

Mary and Joseph had the benefit of an angel who showed up to explain things, but what about the couple contemplating marriage and wondering what the impact will be if one is going to be a pastor? (The issue of clergy couples is beyond the scope of this chapter, but some of the dimensions of congregational expectations are the same.) Without an angel being readily available, what kinds of questions should be asked of each other?

Try these questions: Do you support my decision to be a pastor? If so, how will you express that support? What stresses will the pastoral work put on our relationship? What expectations do we have of each other in the pastoral setting? How will we handle congregational assumptions about our roles? How would the pastoral context influence our life as parents? What stresses will the pastoral work put on our children? Who will decide the church involvements of the non-clergy spouse? What if the faith journey of the non-clergy spouse leads him or her away from the church? What concerns emerge if the pastoral commitment requires us to live in a church-owned parsonage? If either of the couple is divorced, how does that circumstance affect pastoral ministry and family life? In the hurry of congregational life, how do we find time for ourselves? What does Jesus Christ expect of us individually and as a couple?

Any differences a couple might have about shared ministry should be resolved without resorting to the instructions of Deuteronomy 13:6-10. (In order to keep this a G-rated book, I shall not print that passage here. Take a good, deep breath and go read those verses.) More likely than differences between the couple will be differences between congregational understandings and pastor family understandings.

Most congregations have a pastoral advisory committee or a pastor-parish relations committee—a group responsible for keeping healthy the relationship between pastor and pew. This body is an obvious place for interpreting the thoughts of the pastor and family and for clarifying the anticipations of the church members. Discussion with the committee will help keep the matter on top of the table and not the agenda for secret mumbling.

The husband or wife of a pastor is (usually) a layperson who is a member of the pastor's congregation. He or she is subject to the same call to Christian discipleship as any other follower of Jesus. How that call is answered is going to be as varied as the distribution of the gifts of God. "We have gifts that differ according to the grace given to us: prophecy, in proportion to faith; ministry, in ministering; the teacher, in teaching; the exhorter, in exhortation; the giver, in generosity; the leader, in diligence; the compassionate, in cheerfulness" (Romans 12:6-8). Consider: for a congregation to insist that the spouse of a pastor take on a teaching role when that spouse has no gift for teaching is to challenge God's intent for one of God's children. For teaching role, substitute "sing in the choir," "work with the youth," "fill in the pulpit," "go to all the services," "attend staff parties," or "type the bulletin." Make up your own list. What is the spouse's ministry, inaugurated in baptism and filled out in faithful discipleship?

When the writer of Ephesians starts identifying gifts that God gave for ministry, the list includes a powerful word: "some." Some are gifted for apostleship; some are gifted for prophecy; some are gifted for evangelism; some are gifted for pastoral teaching (Ephesians 4:11). Some! The clear implication is that some will have a gift that I do not have. (And I might have a gift that others do not have.) Some! A pastor and spouse should not let others put on them an expectation that God does not have.

Clearly, part of the spouse's call to ministry is the call to be an authentic husband or wife. The main ministry of the wife of a pastor might well be to be the wife of the pastor! The main ministry of the husband of a pastor might well be to be the husband of the pastor! Let me be personal. My wife, Toni, has been the wife of Belton, who happened to be a pastor. Does it make sense to say that she has been not so much the pastor's wife as she has been Belton's wife? If I had owned a hardware store, I think Toni would have been interested in the store; I have been a pastor so it is not surprising that Toni has had interest in the life of the church. But her marital ministry has been to be my wife. (And I am grateful!)

Jesus was dead-on clear that family relationships should not interfere with discipleship (Matthew 19:29, Luke 14:26). I think the same can be said for church relationships. Being a faithful disciple is too important to be left to the whims and pressures of unexamined expectations. Within the family of faith, we are accountable to one another, but that does not mean that others have an order blank for our lives.

None of these reflections is meant to suggest that the spouse of a pastor is beyond offering a service that he or she really does not want to do. Jesus invites us into a diaconal life (John 13:5-8), and holy discernment might well lead one to swallow self-choice and be available for others. The difference between being spiritually abused and being in servant ministry is in who makes the choice.

The apostle Paul tried to clear up some internal issues for the Corinthian church, issues about the roles and behavior of men and women. (In doing so, he created a bit of confusion for our time!) After he offers teachings about hair length for men and women, about women's heads being veiled for prayer, and about the husband being the head of the wife, he comes to a powerful conclusion of equality: "Nevertheless, in the Lord woman is not independent of man or man independent of woman. For just as woman came from man, so man comes through woman; but all things come from God" (1 Corinthians 11:11-12). We are responsible for each other—interdependent—and the gifts each brings to the other come from God. How are we to share those gifts? As one preacher said, "Heaven is not about how much you gained, but about how much you gave."

SOMETHING TO SAY

Thanks, Pat, for caring enough about our music ministry to ask about Yvonne's being in the choir. I'm sure you enjoyed it when Clark Calvin sang in the choir, but if you want to know about Yvonne and the choir, you've asked a question not for the pastor, but for Yvonne! She has to make her own decisions about how to be a disciple, just as you do. Does that make sense?

LET'S KEEP ON TALKING

1. How does the spouse of a pastor know when he or she is appreciated for his or her own self (and not simply as an add-on to the pastor)?

2. What responsibility does any spouse have to be engaged in the work life of her or his spouse?

3. How does any disciple of Jesus discern the gifts given for discipleship?

PRAYER

Gracious and giving God, we confess that life in a marriage is fragile enough without outside pressures bearing in on it. Help us find solid peace and active freedom. Help us become fully who you would have us be and in so doing help us give away the gifts you have given us, through Jesus Christ our Lord. Amen.

?

"WHO ARE YOU GOING TO VOTE FOR, REVEREND?"

THE FEARED QUESTION

Rain on election day usually meant a light turnout of voters, but the long lines at the fire station polling place told a different story. Dripping umbrellas left pools of water everywhere people stood waiting a turn to mark a ballot in the most hotly contested local campaign in memory. The Reverend Simpson Dixon took his place in the procession toward the voting machines.

"Hard to be a good citizen today, isn't it, Reverend?" Phil Travis, a member of Henderson Heights Church, greeted his pastor.

"Hi, Phil," began Simpson Dixon. "You know what they say: if we don't get out and vote on rainy days, the ducks will decide the election!"

"Things got a bit, shall we say, vigorous during the campaign," Phil laughed. "Of course, I'm pretty clear which way we ought to go. Mayor Hunt has been mayor long enough."

The pastor had heard Phil's partisan speech before.

"In fact, I worry about our city if Hunt gets reelected. He keeps wanting to build those apartments for the poor. That is only going to bring more poor to live here."

Simpson Dixon took a deep breath and said, "Well, I guess that by this time tomorrow, we'll know who won."

Phil Travis looked his pastor in the eyes and asked, *"Who are you going to vote for, Reverend?"*

QUICK, FIRST THOUGHTS

If I had gone by the post office first, I would not have gotten stuck in line next to Phil Travis! I feel strongly about this election, but if I say the wrong thing to the wrong person, my ministry could get damaged. I wonder if a pastor has to give up being involved in politics. Phil probably really just wants to know where I stand.

THINKING A BIT MORE ABOUT IT

The Bible has a number of injunctions to believers to be good citizens. Early on, as Moses taught the people of Israel how to be a people of social and religious laws, he said: "You shall not revile God, or curse a leader of your people" (Exodus 22:28). (The King James Version says "the ruler of thy people.")

King Darius enjoined the people "that they may offer pleasing sacrifices to the God of heaven, and pray for the life of the king and his children" (Ezra 6:10).

The advice of Proverbs is:

"My child, fear the LORD and the king,
  and do not disobey either of them." (Proverbs 24:21)

When Pharisees tried to trick Jesus with a question about paying taxes to the government, our Lord replied, "Give therefore to the emperor the things that are the emperor's, and to God the things that are God's" (Matthew 22:21).

Paul argued that one ought to be "subject to the governing authorities" (Romans 13:1) and instructed Timothy to pray "for kings and all who are in high positions, so that we may lead a quiet and peaceable life in all godliness and dignity" (1 Timothy 2:2).

What practical caution does the apostle Paul give through Titus, his "loyal child in the faith" (Titus 1:4)? "Remind them to be subject to rulers and authorities" (3:1).

The weight of these texts seems to suggest almost a blind obedience to the forces of government. Not so!

Consider: "Happy is the nation whose God is the LORD" (Psalm 33:12a). Consider: Any authority that government has, has come from God because "there is no authority except from God" (Romans 13:1b). Consider: "The LORD will reign forever and ever" (Exodus 15:18). Consider: "So acknowledge today and take to heart that the LORD is God in heaven above and on the earth beneath; there is no other" (Deuteronomy 4:39). Consider: Paul quotes, "For it is written,

'As I live, says the LORD, every knee shall bow to me,
  and every tongue shall give praise to God.'" (Romans
14:11)

Consider: James puts government into perspective when he declares, "There is one lawgiver and judge who is able to save and to destroy. So who, then, are you to judge your neighbor?" (James 4:12). Consider: As John moves to close the report of his vision he notes that he hears voices crying out:

> "Hallelujah!
> For the Lord our God
>   the Almighty reigns." (Revelation 19:6b)

The good citizen then is caught in trying to balance respect for and loyalty to government and recognition of the ultimate rule of God. Governments can put a boundary to the harm we do to one another; governments can be part of the way God put the created order together—for relationships; governments can preserve liberty and justice. However! Governments do not always represent God's values of peace (Isaiah 32:17), justice (Micah 6:8), concern for the poor (Proverbs 29:7), reconciliation (2 Corinthians 5:18), respect for all persons (Galatians 3:28), and identification with the vulnerable (Psalm 68:10). A reading of almost any daily newspaper or the review of much of the breaking news distributed on the Internet will be testimony to the failure of governments to be all that God hopes for the societies of God's children. Governments can even put upon its citizens systems that violate the very commands of God. The bottom line was written when Peter and the apostles were confronted with the choice between the authority of government and the authority of God: "We must obey God rather than any human authority" (Acts 5:29).

How does the Christian citizen form an agenda for public policy reflections? For starters, he or she hears the echo of one who introduced himself to his home synagogue by saying:

"The Spirit of the Lord is upon me,
  because he has anointed me
to bring good news to the poor.
He has sent me to proclaim release to the captives
  and recovery of sight to the blind,
  to let the oppressed go free,
to proclaim the year of the Lord's favor." (Luke 4:18-19)

The Christian citizen seeks to make political choices, personal involvements, tax expenditures, and policy decisions that reflect those values named by Jesus. To do so is not to create a theocracy (direct divine rule), but to recognize where God is using the frail instruments of humanity to achieve divine purposes. Christian discipleship is a calling put upon the Christian community, not a formula for governmental practice. The Christian citizen does not work for government to impose Christian faith on others; giving faith is the purview of God and assigned not to government but to the instruments of the church.

Let's assume that the pastor is a Christian citizen. (Understandably, the nuances of these reflections emerge differently in a country where religious freedom is practiced than in a nation where religious freedom is limited.) Does the pastoral role deny the clergyperson the full opportunity to engage in the democratic process? Does the pastoral role block the pastor from any public political posture? What are the boundaries for a pastor in expressing political allegiance? Yard sign? Bumper sticker? Sermon? Study group? Newsletter? Letter to the editor? Candidacy for office?

What is at risk, of course, is the pastoral relationship between pastor and people. When feelings run high (and in most elections they do), it is possible to lose one's pastoral authority if some in the congregation lament the pastor's personal views. Additionally, in the United States, there are considerations of the tax-exempt status of a congregation if its political conversations become partisan and supportive of a particular candidate, rather than being conducted at the level of discussion of values, ethics, and principles. If a pastor becomes a candidate, great care must be taken to separate the political venture from the pastoral task. Few can bring that off.

Does the pastor forfeit the rights of citizenship, the right (in a democracy) to enter fully and freely into the debate and political process? Does a pastor have any more responsibility than any other citizen to make public his or her own political choices? Is the pastor's function so fragile that it might fall apart if political preference is made known? Is it anyone's business how anybody else—including the pastor—plans to vote?

Voting booths have curtains but pulpits do not. A pastor's vote might be secret but the pastor's proclamation is not. Preachers must include the full range of the biblical truth; and that includes a passion for justice, peace, freedom, welfare, and hospitality—concerns that are bound to show up in most elections. But, when the pastor moves beyond the biblical revelation to name names and to indicate how congregants ought to vote, he or she is on a slippery slope.

The voting implications of Christian values are not always apparent. Which candidate offers the best way to help the poor? Which candidate is most likely to improve the chances for peace? Which candidate can advance the likelihood of street safety? Which candidate can sustain long-term educational benefits for all? Which candidate gives the greatest value to life? Which candidate will best preserve personal freedom? Which candidate seems to know what is best for the environment? Even if I figure out which candidate I think best answers those questions, it is probably the case that about 50 percent of the people in the United States do not agree with my decision!

Local elections can be more precarious for the pastor than national elections. Often— particularly in small towns and rural areas—the church membership knows the candidates personally. The candidate for judge is probably somebody's sister! If a candidate is a member of the congregation served by the pastor, matters get even more complicated and exponentially more complicated if the pastor does not plan to vote for that person! It is difficult to keep the matter at an abstract level when personal relationships are involved.

How is a pastor to swim in such treacherous waters? One way is to offer open settings—public forums—to which all points of view are invited. Another way is to stick to asking questions so members have some tools for pondering political choices but are left to the privacy of their consciences for decisions. (After all, a good conscience is a sign of God's prevenient—preceding—universal grace at work.) Another way is to point congregants toward partisan resources—all sides—so members can do their own research and have their own unfiltered encounters with the variety of views. Another way is to have a thematic Bible study on the issues of the day (and leave it to individuals to draw voting conclusions). Another way is to provide copies of denominational statements on various topics (such as the Social Principles of The United Methodist Church).

Another way, of course, is to take that long overdue sabbatical that "just happens" to fall during the election season!

SOMETHING TO SAY

I guess that is something I don't have to ask you, Phil! You have been fully involved in this election and I commend you for being such a good citizen. As a Christian, I think I need to express myself in the voting booth, but as a pastor I am concerned about closing the door on some of the congregation if I make known how I vote. I want to be everybody's pastor, and keeping my vote private is one way I can do that. The rain doesn't seem to be letting up. I hope folks keep coming to vote!

LET'S KEEP ON TALKING

1. Should Christian values be imposed on persons who are not Christians?

2. What is the difference between a pastor's taking a position on an election (choice between candidates) and taking a position on an issue (such as a lottery or a bond referendum)?

3. What is the difference between moral issues and political issues?

PRAYER

Across the years, O God, you have moved among your people to raise up leaders who could with wisdom and courage guide the nations of the world. We must confess that sometimes our own desires and our own hunger for power has made us less sensitive to your will. Grant us now the gift of discernment that we might offer to you the best choices we can make, through Jesus Christ our Lord. Amen.

"WHY ARE YOU LEAVING US FOR ANOTHER CHURCH? DON'T YOU LIKE US?"

THE FEARED QUESTION

Paul Nam thought he had left this sort of question behind when he transferred from a denomination that let individual congregations choose their own pastors. Now he served in a tradition in which the bishop assigned the clergy. But still the question came.

At today's service, the chair of the pastor-parish relations committee announced that in three months there would be a change in pastoral leadership at Trinity Church. Most of the members were not terribly surprised. After all, "Pastor Paul" (as almost all of them called him) had served at Trinity for nine years. These changes simply were part of what it was to be within a system of appointed pastors.

So, when the telephone rang at the parsonage, Pastor Paul

thought it might be another member calling to thank him for his service and to wish him well at his new appointment.

It was not.

"Pastor Paul, this is Mee Cheon Kim. I am not happy that you are leaving Trinity. Did you have any choice in the matter? Were you consulted?"

"Yes, the bishop and I talked about another appointment, a place where he thought I was very much needed."

Mee Cheon Kim's voice rose with a hint of frustration: "As if you are not needed here! Tell me the truth. *Why are you leaving us for another church? Don't you like us?*"

QUICK, FIRST THOUGHTS

Good grief! Wasn't she at church this morning when Ho Kyun Namkung made the announcement? She must know that *itineracy* is part of how we do church! Maybe she is just having trouble dealing with the change, but it's not as if I am the first pastor who ever left Trinity to go to another appointment!

THINKING A BIT MORE ABOUT IT

Even though the apostle Paul did not serve as a local church pastor in the way we know the term, he did frequently reflect on his relationship with particular flocks of God's people. When that tie was broken or threatened or dissolved, there was stress and pain. Notice how often relationships play into his apostolic role.

Almost at the beginning of the letter to the Romans, the apostle says, "For I am longing to see you so that I may share with you some spiritual gift to strengthen you—or rather so that we may be mutually encouraged by each other's faith, both yours and mine" (Romans 1:11-12). Relationship.

When he began his correspondence with the church at Corinth, Paul recognized that some of the faithful were choosing sides among the leaders who had worked with them. "For it has been reported to me by Chloe's people that there are quarrels among you, my brothers and sisters. What I mean is that each of you says, 'I belong to Paul,' or 'I belong to Apollos,' or 'I belong to Cephas,' or 'I belong to Christ.' Has Christ been divided?" (1 Corinthians 1:11-13a). Remembering his ongoing contact with the Corinthian church, Paul closed his second letter by writing, "This is the third time I am coming to you" (2 Corinthians 13:1a). Relationship.

When the apostle addressed the church at Galatia, he made a point of writing some of the letter in his own handwriting, as if he did not want even the work of a secretary to stand between him and the people (Galatians 6:11). He closed his letters to the Colossians and the Thessalonians the same way (Colossians 4:18, 2 Thessalonians 3:17). Relationship.

New Testament scholars often argue that the letter to the Ephesians was actually written not by Paul, but by someone who wrote in behalf of Paul's ministry. One reason given for this conclusion is that the letter contains almost none of the personal relational material that shows up in other Pauline correspondence. This theory underscores the importance of relationships in Paul's work. Relationship.

The Philippian church was generous in support of Paul's gospel-sharing. "You Philippians indeed know that in the early days of the gospel, when I left Macedonia, no church shared with me in the matter of giving and receiving, except you alone" (Philippians 4:15). Relationship.

When the apostle wrote the church at Thessalonica, he remembered gladly important things about that congregation: "work of faith and labor of love and steadfastness of hope in our Lord Jesus Christ" (1 Thessalonians 1:3) and "an example to all the believers in Macedonia and in Achaia" (1 Thessalonians 1:7). Relationship.

Once Paul felt called to leave one place to go to another. "When I came to Troas to proclaim the good news of Christ, a door was opened for me in the Lord; but my mind could not rest because I did not find my brother Titus there. So I said farewell to them and went on to Macedonia" (2 Corinthians 2:12-13). Relationship.

Paul knew how painful it is for a congregation to have some of its leadership depart. "Therefore, when we could bear it no longer, we decided to be left alone in Athens; and we sent Timothy, our brother and co-worker for God" (1 Thessalonians 3:1-2a). Relationship.

Indeed, good, healthy, appropriate relationships are at the heart of the pastoral task. Energy that is spent in fending off unhappy, poor relationships is energy lost to the gospel. It is not surprising, or even unfitting, that a change in pastors stirs a range of emotions within a congregation: loss, disappointment, grief, and—alas—occasionally "hooray!"

What some congregations find hard to accept is that while they are fully part of the universal church of Jesus Christ, their story is not the only story. This may be particularly difficult for local churches in congregational systems of government. Congregations within a connectional polity have many reminders that they share the journey with others. Many independent congregations relate themselves to associations or other links. How do congregations express their common life in Christ?

Paul moved from place to place (look at Acts 16:9-12, for examples). In so doing, he became aware that congregations in City A were tied to congregations in City B. "At present, however, I am going to Jerusalem in a ministry to the saints; for Macedonia and Achaia have been pleased to share their resources with the poor among the saints at Jerusalem" (Romans 15:25-26). When he wrote the church at Corinth, he laid out plans for receiving an offering for the saints in Jerusalem (1 Corinthians 16:1-3). Clearly, the early church recognized that there was a link among the faithful, from city to city, between Jew and Gentile, among the haves and the have nots.

The early church understood that its personnel and its resources were to be shared as best served the cause of the gospel. When a twenty-first-century congregation can understand itself as part of a larger family, it can better appreciate the fact that resources and personnel belong to the whole family and not just to one household. Pastor Nam is not the property of Trinity Church, but is a servant of the whole people of God! In order to determine where he is most needed, one needs to have an overview of the whole church and not just the view of one setting. That judgment might be made by a bishop, a forum of colleagues, or a prayerful inner struggle. The movement of pastors from place to place is an acknowledgment that the church of Jesus Christ exists in many settings.

Certainly, pastoral transfer can occur for a variety of negative reasons: fatigue, empty spirit, loss of financial resources, dispute, lack of vision, moral slippage, boredom, personality clash, leadership style, differing expectations. Sometimes, the change in pastoral leadership cannot come quickly enough for congregation or for pastor.

Classic story no. 427: A pastor and his wife were having a terrible time at Peace Chapel. Nothing seemed to be going right. It was an unhappy pastor-congregation match. One day, the pastor got a call to serve another church. He told his wife, who asked, "What are you going to do about it? Are you going to accept the call?" "Well," he said, "I am going to the study to pray about what to do." His wife answered, "While you are praying, I'm going upstairs and start packing!"

More frequently, the separation of pastor and people is a time of memory of good ministry, sadness at departure, and openness to the tomorrow that God will give both the one who leaves and the congregation that stays. The long-time members are often the key to the change being a smooth one. These "elders" serve as kind of "guarantor figures," persons who can say, "We've done this before and we'll probably do it again. Each change of pastors is a chance to say thanks for the gifts we have had and to claim an opportunity for new gifts."

As hard as it is to do, the pastor who is moving needs to be clear to the congregation that he or she will no longer be in a pastoral relationship with them. It is not because the pastor no longer loves them that this is done; it must be done precisely because the pastor loves them so much that the ties must be broken so the congregation is free to have a mutually enriching relationship with the new pastor. The congregation needs a pastor who is fully its pastor! Remember the words of Paul: "that we may be mutually encouraged by each other's faith" (Romans 1:12b). The congregation needs a pastor who joins them in looking ahead (not one who joins them in looking back). The pastor may have to take the lead in clarifying that her focus will be her new place of service. "Would you want me to give any less to this new church than I have given to you?"

In my own pastoral experience, I have drawn a sharp line upon leaving: no funerals, no weddings, no return to the church unless all former pastors are invited, no visitations in the community. It seems to be the only way to allow my successor to be fully the pastor. Admittedly, it is difficult for me and difficult for my family. At first, it is difficult for a beloved congregation but soon they recognize that they have only one pastor and I am not he. The new pastor can get on with the task of ministry without looking over the shoulder.

If a pastor serves in a system in which others decide the pastoral assignments, he or she might be tempted to blame the powers that be for a change in appointment. The anger of the members is thus diverted from the pastor to the bishop—or to those who make the decision. This might be good strategy for peace and quiet but it is bad strategy for spiritual formation! The pastor is bordering on (if indeed not toppling into) lying. Even if a pastor disagrees with the proposed move, he serves neither self nor congregation nor the larger church well by foisting blame on others. After all, the pastor has willingly agreed to be part of a system in which others decide the assignments. Most polity has built in some patterns of consultation, both with the clergy and with the local church. These consultations do not imply agreement all around, but they do provide an opportunity for input, distinctive factors, and comment.

Often forgotten in the troubled waters of a pastoral change is this question: *How is Jesus Christ best served?* The question is not as narrow as *What is best for me?* or even *What is best for this congregation?* The measuring stick has to be the church of Jesus Christ and the Lord whom that church serves.

SOMETHING TO SAY

Do I love this congregation? Indeed I do! Will I miss this congregation? Indeed I will! What do I think of this move? God is not through with it yet because God has a good tomorrow for me and for Trinity Church. You and I are blessed to be in connection with other congregations who love and serve God. Somewhere, there is another congregation that is sad at losing its pastor, but that pastor is coming here. You can help that new pastor be happy about being here. Can you think of some ways you can do that?

LET US KEEP ON TALKING

1. How should decisions be made about pastoral changes?
2. Under what circumstances should a former pastor return to a parish?
3. How can a congregation say good-bye to a departing pastor and welcome a new pastor?

PRAYER

What is the tomorrow to which you call us, O God? Even when I do not know its shape or the place it will call home, I trust that you will be there. Thank you for the blessings of pastor and people. Thank you for giving us the larger family of Christ. Thank you for the unfailing mercy that can touch our disappointments with hope, our excitement with energy, and our uncertainties with promise, through Jesus Christ our Lord. Amen.

QUESTION SEVEN

"WHY DO YOU PICK HYMNS THAT NO ONE LIKES?"

THE FEARED QUESTION

The first couple of times that Brenda Martin spoke to her pastor about the music, she did so in a teasing voice. "I bet you picked that hymn just so you wouldn't have to listen to me sing!" she laughed.

Last Sunday, Pastor Kenneth O'Reilly knew he had worked hard to plan the worship service. The keyboard player had chosen music that hit the lectionary theme perfectly. The liturgical dance was beautifully done by two youth from the congregation. When the pastor offered a time with young disciples, the children had clapped with glee as hand puppets had made the Gospel reading come alive. The sermon—well, who was he to say?—was a clear and contemporary unfolding of the biblical revelation. And the hymns had brought the whole service together, each one embracing the biblical theme for the day.

This time when Ms. Martin spoke to the pastor, she was not smiling. "I come to church to worship God and to enjoy being with friends," she said. "Week after week, you try to get us to sing things you know, and pay no attention to whether we sing it or not. *Why do you pick hymns that no one likes?*"

QUICK, FIRST THOUGHTS

And, Ms. Martin, just where did you get your theological classes in worship leadership? I am a trained professional and I know what is best for worship. I guess she is just longing for what is comfortable for her in worship. I should not be too hard on her because I think she means well. But how will I ever explain these theological nuances so she gets it?

THINKING A BIT MORE ABOUT IT

Worship is a defining characteristic of the church. Some persons have gone so far as to say that worship is the only significant thing separating church from civic club. Worship is at the core of the life of the gathered community. Public worship is, as John Wesley indicated, a means of God's grace.

It is not surprising, therefore, that issues around worship are often the most heartfelt concerns within a congregation. After all, the services of worship are probably the most widely visible activities in the life of the church. When people speak of "going to church," they almost always mean going to the worship service.

If worship is at the heart of the gathered Christian community, music is at the heart of worship. Music both reflects
and generates feelings. Music adds another dimension to the
written or spoken word, much as a smile adds a dimension
to the greeting "Good morning." Music provides a rhythmic
experience that connects with the heart's regular pace. Music
reinforces (or challenges) the tone of text. Music without
words leaves room for personal engagement in a way that
words without music do not always do. (Ask a group the
meaning of words and the answers will be pretty much the
same; ask the same group the meaning of a piece of music
and the answers will run a wide range.) Is it any wonder that
Brenda Martin was upset when "her" music went missing!

Music is a thread throughout the biblical journey. When
Laban asked Jacob why Jacob had sneaked away, Laban
said: "Why did you flee secretly and deceive me and not tell
me? I would have sent you away with mirth and songs,
with tambourines and lyre" (Genesis 31:27).

Music is a mark of biblical celebration. When Israel remembered how God delivered them from slavery in Egypt,
they sang:

> Then Moses and the Israelites sang this song to the LORD:
> "I will sing to the LORD, for he has triumphed gloriously;
>   horse and rider he has thrown into the sea."
> (Exodus 15:1)

Music is the spontaneous expression of biblical joy. After
King Jabin of Canaan was defeated by the Israelites, the vic-
tors broke into song:

> Then Deborah and Barak son of Abinoam sang on that
> day, saying:
>   "When locks are long in Israel,

when the people offer themselves willingly—
bless the LORD!

"Hear, O kings; give ear, O princes;
  to the LORD I will sing,
  I will make melody to the LORD, the God of Israel."
                                      (Judges 5:1-3)

Music is at the heart of Old Testament worship. The Psalms bring that music into one collection. For example:

Sing to God, sing praises to his name;
  lift up a song to him who rides upon the clouds—
his name is the LORD—
  be exultant before him. (Psalm 68:4)

Music is part of the institution of the Lord's Supper. "'Take; this is my body.'...'This is my blood of the covenant, which is poured out for many.'...When they had sung the hymn, they went out to the Mount of Olives" (Mark 14:22c, 24b, 26).

Music is the blend of thought and emotion for the apostle Paul. "I will sing praise with the spirit, but I will sing praise with the mind also" (1 Corinthians 14:15b).

Music is a biblical sign of being filled with the Spirit. "But be filled with the Spirit, as you sing psalms and hymns and spiritual songs among yourselves, singing and making melody to the Lord in your hearts" (Ephesians 5:18b-19).

Music is the sound that is heard at God's throne in heaven. "And I heard a voice from heaven like the sound of many waters and like the sound of loud thunder; the voice I heard was like the sound of harpists playing on their harps, and they sing a new song before the throne" (Revelation 14:2-3a).

With music so patently in the fiber of the biblical account of the relationship of God's people with God, one should be ready for music to be in the fabric of today's church life. The selection of hymns is an important link to that biblical tradition. Hymns, perhaps more than anthems or instrumental selections, belong to all the people. An anthem or an organ voluntary or a solo or a praise band's gathering music is presented as a gift to God in behalf of the people; a hymn is an offering presented by the people themselves.

A favorite seminary professor said that he once had a church member who told him, "If they are going to 'sing a new song' in heaven [Revelation 14:3a], then I'm not going." That concern may well be what motivated Brenda Martin to dispute Pastor O'Reilly's hymn choices!

What are the factors in the selection of hymns? (1) A hymn should be faithful to the biblical theme of the day. (Pastors following the lectionary often have source books to help with those choices.) (2) A hymn should come at an appropriate place within the service. (Musicians using praise songs and choruses often work hard to have a sequence of music that leads worshipers through gathering, praise, confession, forgiveness, hearing, offering, and so forth.) (3) A hymn should be in the musical range of the congregation. (A little pre-service practice—or rehearsal at a mid-week church program—will help a congregation feel more comfortable with hymns that are less familiar or that test the musical readiness of the congregants.) (4) A hymn should be theologically sound. (Many learned about the atonement from the traditional "Old Rugged Cross" or the contemporary "Embrace the Cross"; our theology is shaped by what we sing.) (5) A hymn should give people a faith voice. (This means that hymn selection should include both hymns that move us to new faith places and hymns that remind us of older faith journeys.) (6) A hymn ought to be defendable. (It is important for a worship leader to be clear on the motive in choosing a hymn: the words are on target for this service, we needed to start with a hymn that could be sung with vigor, several people requested it, it is a poetic arrangement of the Bible lesson, it offers a different perspective on an old truth, it's a favorite.)

When the worship hymn mixture seems to omit some hymns or songs that people wish to sing, some congregations begin the gathering time with a chance for congregants to name what is to be sung. This "hymn fest" can precede the regular worship time and can provide an informal balance to services with a high liturgical content.

If a congregant complains that "we don't sing the *old* songs," what is often meant is "We don't sing songs that have emotional content for me." Most of the really old hymns of the church were written in Latin or Greek, and it is not likely that members are concerned about these "oldies." "How Great Thou Art" is often thought of as a hymn of the ages, but it is only about fifty years old. "The Old Rugged Cross" (often requested by older congregations) is actually a twentieth-century hymn.

Persons whose faith trek has been via contemporary praise songs will soon be clamoring for the praise songs they first knew: the "old songs" written ten years ago. It does not take long for music to get labeled "outdated"! If a member of the worshiping community complains about "having to sing those dreary hymns," what might be meant is "those kinds of words and tunes do not represent my experience." Persons new to the faith family do not always find classic hymns very accessible.

From time to time, the local congregation of which I am a part sings "Jesus loves me! This I know, for the Bible tells me so"—the classic children's worship song. I enjoy singing it. But if my faith expedition has not traveled beyond my five-year-old faith, I would have to confess that I must have missed some messages God sent me. It is good to recall the points of passage on one's spiritual path, but it denies that we have a living God if we continue to live only in that past. God is still alive; why aren't we?

A protest that we sing hymns nobody knows often implies that "no one else knows a hymn that I do not know." Even in the smallest congregations, there will be a variety of religious voyages and a variety of musical tastes and a variety of hymn preferences. One (and this includes the pastor) should be cautious in making assumptions that "no one" knows or likes a particular hymn.

Dealing with church music is not an occasion for drawing a heavy theological or esoteric artistic line in the sand. It is a time for sensitivity, awareness, and a recognition of the value of growth in faith experiences. After all, we are singing unto the Lord!

SOMETHING TO SAY

Brenda, I appreciate that question because it lets me know that you care deeply about one of the most important times in our congregation's life: when we gather to worship. I try to pick hymns that we can sing—I guess I do miss the mark on that occasionally—and I seek to find hymns that fit the service on a particular day. Of course, different people know different hymns. What is one of your favorites?

LET'S KEEP ON TALKING

1. If you had to choose between choosing hymns and songs that people can sing easily or choosing hymns and songs that are theologically sound, which would (should?) you choose?

2. How do you evaluate the theological content of a hymn?

3. What hymn are you humming in your head right now?

PRAYER

"Praise the LORD!
Sing to the LORD a new song,
   his praise in the assembly of the faithful.
Let [us] be glad in [our] Maker;
   let the children of Zion rejoice in their King.
Let them praise his name with dancing,
   making melody to him with tambourine and
      lyre."

[Psalm 149:1-3]

We give you thanks, O God, for giving us voice—both voice of our hearts and voice of our lips. We offer our song to you in praise, in repentance, in listening, and in serving, through Jesus Christ, our Lord. Amen.

QUESTION EIGHT

"WHY DO WE KEEP SENDING OFF MONEY FOR MISSIONS?"

THE FEARED QUESTION

Anson Holloway seemed calm enough when he spoke up at the finance committee meeting: "Doesn't the Bible say that charity begins at home?"

"Uh, I'm not sure," the committee chairperson replied. "Let's ask the pastor."

The Reverend Ms. Olivet began slowly, trying not to offend. "Let me see if I can reach back into my college English course. It was, if I am not mistaken, Sir Thomas Browne who coined the phrase sometime in the seventeenth century. So, I guess 'Charity begins at home' is not a biblical saying."

"Well, it ought to be," laughed Mr. Holloway. "We've been trying to make sense of this church budget for almost an hour and a half and all I have to say is that as long as we have all this missions money in here, we are not going to get the budget balanced." He paused and laughingly added, "Unless, of course, you don't need all your salary, pastor!"

The chairperson smiled. "Has it come to that? Is the only choice between the pastor's salary and money for missions?"

"You can't get blood out of a turnip," Anson Holloway continued. "We are not exactly First Church, you know! We only had thirty-five in worship last Sunday."

"What percentage of our budget is for missions?" inquired a youth member of the committee.

Mr. Holloway said, "Maybe another way of asking the question is, *Why do we keep sending off money for missions?*"

QUICK, FIRST THOUGHTS

What a strange question for a Christian to ask! I wonder if Anson has slept through the first forty years of his faith, kind of a spiritual Rip Van Winkle! I hate it when folks like him get on the finance committee. I don't know how I can keep my cool when I answer him. But the truth is that I've run into that question in every church I have served. Alas.

THINKING A BIT MORE ABOUT IT

The church is the mission of Jesus Christ in the world. As the Body of Christ (Ephesians 1:22-23, Colossians 1:18), the church is the mission of Christ. In that sense, the church does not have a mission; the church is the mission.

Our Lord came that his sheep "may have life, and have it abundantly" (John 10:10). That is the mission. Our Lord came "that everyone who believes in him may not perish but may have eternal life" (John 3:16). That is the mission. Our Lord came that the thirsty might have drink, the hungry might have food, the naked might have clothes, the imprisoned might have friends, the sick might have healing, the stranger might have companions (Matthew 25:31-46). That is the mission. Our Lord came that the poor might hear good news, the captives might know freedom, the oppressed might have liberty, the blind might see, and all might know of God's favor (Luke 4:18-19). That is the mission. Our Lord said:

> " 'Worship the Lord your God
> and serve only him.' " (Matthew 4:10)

That is the mission.

The church is that mission. "Missions" is simply one way the church is mission. Missions is the intentional outreach in the name of Jesus Christ to those who need light shined in their darkness. Of course, all of us have shadow places in our lives that need light, but missions is when the light shines from us, not on us. (We can indeed be the object of the missional outreach of others—indeed, let us hope we are!) Traditionally, the church refers to its own spiritual formation and growth as ministry and refers to that offer to others as mission.

In 1956, the Methodist Youth Clubs of the British Methodist Church developed seven principles for their work. One of those basics was "live on a large map" (John Munsey Turner, *Modern Methodism in England 1932-1998* [Peterborough, Great Britain: Epworth Press, 1998], p. 76). That is a vital description of the expansiveness of the gospel imperative. A large map! The writer of Ephesians puts it this way: "For [Christ] is our peace; in his flesh he has made both groups into one and has broken down the dividing wall, that is, the hostility between us" (Ephesians 2:14). Jesus Christ has put us on a large map.

Because of Christ, the usual human boundaries of race, space, and place have been put aside. The mission that is the church has no border at which it should stop. The need in the Sudan is as close as the need in Nebraska, and the need in Nebraska is as close as the need in Cambodia, and the need in Cambodia is as close as—well, you get the picture.

Jesus knew that such mission is as dangerous as it is unreserved: "See, I am sending you out like sheep into the midst of wolves; so be wise as serpents and innocent as doves" (Matthew 10:16). Mission takes wisdom, discernment of major proportions. What is the best use of resources? How do we disperse personnel? How do we discover needs? How do we set priorities? How do we make sure that our mission work is partnership and not simply a one-way street? Local churches that are in global connectional systems or that have links around the world are in the best position to make these decisions wisely.

How did Jesus send forth disciples for mission?

> Now the eleven disciples went to Galilee, to the mountain to which Jesus had directed them. When they saw him, they worshiped him; but some doubted. And Jesus came and said to them, "All authority in heaven and on earth has been given to me. Go therefore and make disciples of all nations, baptizing them in the name of the Father and of the Son and of the Holy Spirit, and teaching them to obey everything that I have commanded you. And remember, I am with you always, to the end of the age." (Matthew 28:16-20)

Part of the missional task is to invite others to the missional task. How is missions money part of that undertaking? When Jesus commissioned the disciples to "go therefore and make disciples of all nations" (Matthew 28:19a), he included in the charge that they were to teach "them to obey everything that I have commanded" (Matthew 28:20a). Those commandments include feeding, clothing, visiting, healing, and passing on the good news. Have we made disciples as Jesus commanded? The answer is in the obedience of those whom we have taught, their obedience to the commands of Jesus. The question becomes: Does missions money help that happen?

There is plenty of need on our doorstep. Why do we send resources to far places? First, we do so because Jesus told us to (Luke 24:47). Second, we do so because the early church modeled borderless ministry (Acts 16:9-10). Third, we do so to remind us that God's call is to "shine like stars in the [whole] world" (Philippians 2:15b). To focus mission entirely on our own neighborhood is to miss those three dimensions of the gospel assignment.

Certainly there is a place for local missions, particularly among the "other" in our midst. Our Lord paused to wash the feet of his own disciples (John 13:3-5) even as he prepared to give his life for all humanity. His own walking mission touched those he met (Matthew 9:27-31, Mark 1:31, Luke 13:10-13, for quick examples). Our mission also should touch those we meet. Local food bank? Habitat for Humanity? Rescue mission shelter? Neighborhood poverty? Community violence? Housing issues? The appeal for global missions is not in any way intended to close the door on local missions. The appeal for global missions is to remind us that a hungry child in Africa is as hungry as a hungry child in your state. A person living in Russia without accepting our Lord is as broken as a person living on my street without accepting our Lord.

Transnational mission partnerships offer gifts to all concerned. Each can provide balance to the other. Out my window in Bahama, North Carolina, I can see things that you cannot see if you are reading this in Moscow, Idaho, or in Moscow, Russia. But then you can see things in Moscow (or Moscow) that I cannot see in Bahama. All of us see better if we tell one another what we are seeing! A global mission reflects a world of "Parthians, Medes, Elamites, and residents of Mesopotamia, Judea and Cappadocia, Pontus and Asia, Phrygia and Pamphylia, Egypt and the parts of Libya belonging to Cyrene, and visitors from Rome, both Jews and proselytes, Cretans and Arabs" (Acts 2:9-11a). Global mission is Pentecost mission.

Money "sent off for missions" is not really "sent off." Such funds are still going to a place and a people for whom God has concern. Do we have any other measuring stick for making missional judgments? Almost without fail, when persons have visited mission sites, they come away with a deep fondness for the mission. Church members who go on mission work teams return as the most excited and energized about missional support. It is easy to vote down a line in a budget, but it is far more difficult to say no to Jorge Garcia, to Bettye Ellison, to Vladimir Fradkov, to Sia Fatuma—that is, to a person one has met. Global missions may be about a different room in the family house, but it is still home.

In John's strange vision of heaven, he sees angels at "the four corners of the earth" (Revelation 7:1a). In his dream of the New Jerusalem, there are gates for the north, gates for the south, gates for the east, and gates for the west (Revelation 21:13). John sees a city with length and width equal in all directions (Revelation 21:16). From all perspectives, John's image of God's coming reign is one that gives equivalent import to each corner of the new heaven and the new earth. We begin to anticipate God's new world when we live out of a global context, when we understand the gospel to be as wide and as far-reaching as God's grace: to all four corners!

When the apostle Peter struggled about what should be the breadth of his ministry, God sent a vision of a large sheet coming down from heaven, filled with all sorts of things that Peter had thought to be unclean, not right for a faithful Jew to eat. Yet the voice of the vision said, "Get up, Peter; kill and eat." This message opened the door for Peter to share the gospel with the Gentile Cornelius. Peter saw the expansion of his proclamation to the Gentiles because "I truly understand that God shows no partiality." (This account is in Acts 10.) In that sheet today might not be "all kinds of four-footed creatures and reptiles and birds of the air" (as Peter saw); instead, in that sheet today might be people of all nations, persons on various faith journeys, those of varying mental capacity, men and women in a range of financial security, humans who acknowledge a particular sexual orientation—and God invites us to say with Peter, "I truly understand that God shows no partiality."

SOMETHING TO SAY

Anson, you obviously feel strongly about this. Let me tell you where I am coming from on the matter of missions money. My feeling is that the church does not draw boundary lines in the same way as governments or other institutions do. When we are at our best, we do not have very much of a "we/they" mindset.

The earth is the LORD's and all that is in it,
  the world, and those who live in it. (Psalm 24:1)

That doesn't leave much room for putting all of God's money behind our walls. Does that make sense?

LET'S KEEP ON TALKING

1. How does a local church decide between "keeping the lights on" and giving money for missions?

2. What gifts are given affluent congregations by those with fewer financial resources?

3. How important is it that recipients of mission resources (food for the hungry, for example) know that the gift is in the name of Jesus Christ?

PRAYER

God of here and there, you for whom there are no near and far places, help us recognize as sisters and brothers all those whom you have created. Give us such love of our own homes that we wish the same joy for others. Give us such concern for our own people that we are eager to have that concern for the broader family. Give us such delight in your presence that we shall with delight spread the news of your love, through Jesus Christ our Lord. Amen.

"WHY CAN'T WE USE CHRISTMAS RED ON THE ALTAR TABLE DURING DECEMBER?"

THE FEARED QUESTION

R oger Singleton was changing the paraments at Piedmont Church. He said to himself, "We've got to get a worship committee in place—an altar guild or something—so I don't have to keep on doing this." He stepped back to look at the cloths on the pulpit and the Communion table.

"Well done, Reverend Singleton!" a voice called out from the back of the sanctuary.

The pastor turned and saw Bill and Gladys Cox, long-time members of Piedmont Church and the sorts who were willing to do whatever needed to be done at the church (and famous for saying what they were thinking). "Are you putting up the Christmas decorations?"

Pastor Singleton took a deep breath and reminded himself that he was new as pastor of Piedmont Church and that following the church season calendar was new for Piedmont Church. "Not exactly," he said. "These Sundays before Christmas are called the Sundays of Advent. It is still four weeks until Christmas."

"Yes," Gladys said, "but all the stores in town are beginning to look so festive. Don't you think the church ought to look bright and Christmassy? I don't know about that purple; it's kind of a downer. *Why can't we use Christmas red on the altar table during December?*"

QUICK, FIRST THOUGHTS

I've got a long way to go with getting these people up to speed on the right colors to use for the paraments. And I thought Gladys and Bill were pretty much on board with my teaching about the church year. Red during December? Mercy, if any of my preacher colleagues came by and saw that, they would laugh me all the way to the North Pole! Besides, red does not go well with my brown eyes! But I know the Singletons mean well and want the best for the church.

THINKING A BIT MORE ABOUT IT

Some issues that come before a pastor are not life-and-death matters for the gospel. The question addressed in this chapter is one of those. It does provide an opportunity to bring clarity to the full gospel message, but it is not likely to block (or enhance!) anyone's access to heaven.

Primitive people might have used only day and night as a way of measuring the passing of time. Later, observations of the moon led to putting together blocks of time tied to the stages of the moon. (The word "month" comes from the Old English word for moon.) Putting these months together led to the development of a lunar year and later a solar year (the earth completing a revolution around the sun).

Christians latched onto the seven-day week cycle as a way to remember Christ's resurrection on the first day of the week. Gradually, other special days of Christian memory were added in order to recall and celebrate the major ingredients in the gospel story. That way of annually retelling the church's story continues to evolve and dissolve. (For example, a United Methodist effort to establish a season of Kingdomtide never caught on in the ecumenical community and has been abandoned now by most United Methodist congregations.)

Over the centuries, each of the seasons of the church year (Advent, Christmas, Lent, and Easter, for example) came to be expressed by a particular color. It was not always like that. When churches first began to use fabrics for clergy vestments and stoles and began to hang cloth from the pulpit, lectern, and Lord's table, the season was represented not by a color but by the quality of the fabric. Easter and Christmas got the finest fabric regardless of its color. (For more on this practice, see Laurence Hull Stookey, *Calendar: Christ's Time for the Church* [Nashville: Abingdon Press, 1996], p. 155.)

In the sixteenth century, the Roman Catholic Council of

Trent tried to bring order to the multifarious colors used for seasonal observances. Difficulties developed because the same color might signify a different theme according to the culture. For example, white is sometimes used to capture the joy of Easter and Christmas, but there are Asian cultures in which white is a symbol for mourning. The rationale for determining which color to use for liturgical seasons may be no better than the interpretation given. (Someone once said that if you have to explain a symbol, it is not much of a symbol.)

Does it matter if Church A uses color differently from Church B? In the ultimate scheme of things, probably not. There is, however, something akin to haughtiness that leads one part of the family to ignore the patterns and emphases of the rest of the family. A congregation that goes its own way in the use of church seasonal colors may in some way cut itself off from the central flow of the full community's life and story. The bottom line would be that any vast variance from common practice ought to be done with serious thought and not with casual boredom.

It is not likely that the kingdom of God will screech to a halt if a local church "messes up" on the correct seasonal color. There is a chance, however, that such a congregation might miss some central theme of the gospel account. The colors are reminders and if we are not reminded we might forget!

Secular use of color sometimes contrasts with church practice. (To have the church distinct from the surrounding culture is not a bad thing!) Red and green at Christmas, yellow at Easter, and orange at Halloween (All Saints Eve) are efforts within the culture to trigger memory and observance. The Christian community is not always responding to the same values as the world around it, so it is not surprising that the church might choose colors that are different from those used in the business arena.

There are generally accepted practices that cross ecumenical lines (Denominations often produce guidelines for their own participants, noting any variances from the common use of color.) Here are some of those general conventions regarding liturgical colors for the Christian year.

Advent: Purple (violet) is used both as a color of repentance—how else do we prepare for the coming of Christ?—and as a color of royalty (because the dyes for making purple cloth were extraordinarily expensive (Acts 16:14). In recent years, during Advent some congregations have begun to use blue, a color of hope, moving away from a penitential theme into a theme of expectancy. Blue is sometimes identified with Mary, the mother of Jesus.

Christmas: White or gold are seen as celebration colors, capturing the joy of this festive season. (In church custom, the color red does not represent Christmas, but carries other imagery, including the flames of the Holy Spirit and the blood of Christ.)

Epiphany: This season begins with the commemoration of the coming of the wise men to the young child Jesus, and the Sundays that follow are called Sundays after Epiphany. These Sundays are labeled "ordinary time," not because they are routine and undistinguished, but because the Sundays are counted with ordinals—numbers such as third Sunday after Epiphany, fifth Sunday after Epiphany. Green, a mark of growth, is used during this season of steady nourishment and extension of the gospel story.

Lent: Because these days before Easter (not including Sundays) are seen as penitential preparation for Easter, the color purple is used. (These Sundays are called Sundays *in* Lent, not Sundays *of* Lent, because the resurrection day is not considered part of the Lenten cycle.)

Easter: During this season—more than just Easter Sunday—the festive colors of gold or white are customary.

Day of Pentecost: Red is a reminder of Pentecostal flames (Acts 2:3). Some churches use red on anniversaries and special occasions of remembrance as a way of recalling the blood of the martyrs, all those before us who have given life in faithfulness. Because ordinations are about the gift of the Holy Spirit, most traditions use red on those occasions. The Sundays after Pentecost are called ordinary time (see explanation above) and green, the color of growth, is employed.

Christ the King: As the church year comes full rotation, it ends with Christ the King Sunday, with white and gold being the color symbols.

There is a host of variations on these broad strokes: Ash Wednesday, Good Friday, Holy Thursday, Transfiguration Sunday, All Saints Sunday, and so forth. The very fact that there are so many subtle shifts in the usual patterns suggests that the colors are most helpful when they remind and teach, when they help congregations focus on the unfolding gospel calendar, and when they assure a balanced and full telling of the good news. Otherwise, the colors are just decoration.

The Bible does not prescribe particular colors for particular times, but the Scripture has many examples of color (sometimes named as the color of precious stones) being used to magnify a point or to illustrate a teaching:

> I am about to set your stones in antimony,
>   and lay your foundations with sapphires.
> I will make your pinnacles of rubies. (Isaiah 54:11-12a)

> ...the wings of a dove covered with silver,
>   its pinions with green gold. (Psalm 68:13bc)

She is not afraid for her household when it snows,
   for all her household are clothed in crimson.
She makes herself coverings;
   her clothing is fine linen and purple. (Proverbs 31:
21-22)

They stripped [Jesus] and put a scarlet robe on him.
(Matthew 27:28)

"Then I saw a great white throne and the one who sat
on it."   (Revelation 20:11a)

The wall is built of jasper, while the city is pure gold,
clear as glass. The foundations of the wall of the city are
adorned with every jewel; the first was jasper, the second sapphire, the third agate, the fourth emerald, the
fifth onyx, the sixth carnelian, the seventh chrsysolite,
the eighth beryl, the ninth topaz, the tenth chrysoprase,
the eleventh jacinth, the twelfth amethyst. (Revelation
21:18-20)

Though your sins are like scarlet,
   they shall be like snow;
though they are red like crimson,
   they shall become like wool. (Isaiah 1:18bc)

Thoughtful use of color in the sanctuary is important because worship is important. Whatever enhances the worship of God is significant. There is a danger, however, that
the enhancement might be seen as more nearly essential
than the thing (the One?) that is enhanced! As we work to
make appropriate choices about liturgical colors, we do well
to hear an echo of the prophet Amos:

I hate, I despise your festivals,
   and I take no delight in your solemn assemblies.
                                (Amos 5:21)

If we lose sight of the gospel to which the colors point, we do well to hear Paul's caution to the church in Galatia: "You are observing special days, and months, and seasons, and years. I am afraid that my work for you may have been wasted" (Galatians 4:10).

None of these warnings is intended to diminish the value of anything that points to the full gospel message—and liturgical colors do that. The caution is "do not confuse the wrapping paper with the present!" Folklore says that just before the Russian revolution, the hierarchy of the Russian Orthodox Church was spending its time arguing about liturgical colors, oblivious to the changing world around it.

That story represents the call to watchfulness. When debate about "the hues of heaven" diverts us from who we are called to be, it is a bad thing. When the use of colors points the church toward worship and mission and service and growth, it is a good thing.

SOMETHING TO SAY

Good morning, Gladys and Bill! I agree with you: it gets complicated when church talk is different from the way the rest of the world talks! We put purple on the pulpit and Table during these Sundays before Christmas to remind us that the new baby is a king and to teach us that the King is coming again to establish his reign! Purple is often seen as the color of kings—of royalty—because years ago it was so expensive to make purple dye that only royalty could afford it. More to the point, perhaps, is the value of church tradition; we here at Piedmont Church are part of something bigger than we are. That does get a bit knotty, doesn't it? Do you think it would help if I spent a little time Sunday talking about this?

LET'S KEEP ON TALKING

1. Some persons feel that using the color "white" to represent joy and purity is demeaning to people of color. How do you feel about that?

2. If the church is trying to reach the world around it with the gospel, why should the church use symbols (colors) that the world does not understand?

3. How is color used to express attitudes and themes outside the church?

PRAYER

Across the years you have come to your people, and we are grateful. You are even coming to us from tomorrow! And we are grateful! We offer to you our pale reflections upon the rich rainbow of your presence. Even as we recall the seasons of your gifts, we reach for that eternity from which you come to us; and we claim it even now, through Jesus Christ our Lord. Amen.

"ARE ALL ACTS OF GOD ACTS OF GOD?"

THE FEARED QUESTION

The bottom of the third inning of the high school baseball game did not seem to be a likely spot for a heavy theological discussion. There were two outs, the bases were loaded, and Jose Ruiz was coming to bat: the best hitter the Beacons had.

That was the moment that Bryan Johnson chose to ask his pastor about the weather.

"It has surely rained a lot lately," Bryan began. "And more in some places than here."

"Yep," Pastor Lucas responded. Then, trying to get focused again on the game, he added, "The field is kind of slow with the grass so tall and the ground so soft."

Bryan tried again. "That much rain is too much. Crops get hurt. Bad roofs leak. And in some places, things even get washed away."

Two balls and a strike on Jose Ruiz. "Indeed," said the pastor. "A lot of rain," turning his attention back to the left-hander on the mound.

"I'll tell you what I'm really thinking," Bryan continued. "Rain is supposed to be an act of God, isn't it?"

"Wow!" exclaimed Pastor Lucas. "Did you see that curve! It's a good thing it missed the plate."

"I'm serious," Bryan protested. "Does God cause floods like the one in the next state over? If God causes rain and floods, I have to wonder: *Are all acts of God acts of God?*"

QUICK, FIRST THOUGHTS

Why doesn't he stop bugging me while I'm watching the game? What is eating at him so bad right now about the floods? Three men on base is no time for theological discussion! Bryan must be feeling vulnerable because of his own farm. I guess I can read about the game in the paper. Oh, well.

THINKING A BIT MORE ABOUT IT

If God gets the credit for good weather, why should not God get the blame for bad weather? Hurricanes. Tornados. Earthquakes. Floods. Wind storms. Tsunamis. The biblical writers are fairly clear that all of these items are in God's repertoire.

> For I know that the LORD is great;
>   our LORD is above all gods.
> Whatever the LORD pleases he does,
>   in heaven and on earth,
>   in the seas and all deeps.

He it is who makes the clouds rise at the end of the earth;
   he makes lightnings for the rain
   and brings out the wind from his storehouses.
                                          (Psalm 135:5-7)

The Lord, GOD of hosts . . .
who builds his upper chambers in the heavens,
   and founds his vault upon the earth;
who calls for the waters of the sea,
   and pours them out upon the surface of the earth—
the LORD is his name. (Amos 9:5a, 6)

As soon as [Moses] finished speaking all these words, the
ground under [the people of Korah] was split apart. The
earth opened its mouth and swallowed them up, along
with their households—everyone who belonged to Korah
and all their goods. . . . And fire came out from the LORD
and consumed the two hundred fifty men offering the in-
cense. (Numbers 16:31-32a, 35)

"When he opened the sixth seal, I looked, and there came
a great earthquake; the sun became black as sackcloth,
the full moon became like blood, and the stars of the sky
fell to the earth." (Revelation 6:12-13a)

"For in seven days I will send rain on the earth for forty
days and forty nights; and every living thing that I have
made I will blot out from the face of the ground." (Genesis 7:4)

In these accounts, we get a picture of a God sitting at the
controls of a giant weather wheel, spinning it to suit God's
own plan. But Jesus challenged the notion that God is fickle
in dispensing the support and the judgments of weather,
"for he makes his sun rise on the evil and on the good, and
sends rain on the righteous and on the unrighteous"
(Matthew 5:45b).

In fact, Jesus himself took on the forces of nature when
a storm threatened his disciples:

A great windstorm arose, and the waves beat into the boat, so that the boat was already being swamped. But [Jesus] was in the stern, asleep on the cushion; and [the disciples] woke him up and said to him, "Teacher, do you not care that we are perishing?" He woke up and rebuked the wind, and said to the sea, "Peace! Be still!" Then the wind ceased, and there was a dead calm.... And they were filled with great awe and said to one another, "Who then is this, that even the wind and the sea obey him"? (Mark 4:37-39, 41)

In Acts 27, Luke records an account of a terrible tempest that threatened the lives of all on a ship that transported Paul (as a prisoner). In an effort to keep the boat afloat, the crew tossed overboard cargo and tackle and food. Paul told the crew that an angel of God had assured him that all would be safe. Their escape to land was treacherous but successful. In this description, the storm shows no respect for souls or ships, but the providence of God delivered those God promised to save. (The account spills over into Acts 28.)

Three biblical approaches to natural disasters have emerged: (a) God does what God wants to with the weather, (b) God distributes the weather without regard to who is affected, (c) God lets the weather "do its thing" but provides care for those whom God protects. Which is it?

Insurance companies (and others who need to define such things) generally refer to natural disasters as "acts of God." (I don't recall seeing an insurance policy that identified sunshine and warmth and pleasant days with light showers as being acts of God!) What is an act of God? An event without human intervention. Usually, the popular use of the term "act of God" describes an occurrence of such magnitude that even reasonable preparation or foresight could not affect it.

God has brought into being all of the created order (Genesis 1:1–2:4). All things were created through the eternal Christ and for him (Colossians 1:16b). Did God act as a watchmaker God who just set the creation into motion and then stepped aside to let it tick? Is it possible that God no longer intervenes in the affairs of nature? Now that we understand that wind currents and ocean warmth and atmospheric conditions set our weather into motion, do we any longer need God as part of nature's picture? ("Sure, God did a great job creating a beautiful universe, but what has God done for us lately?")

If God constantly played with the throttles of the weather machines, we would lose the consistency and predictability of natural principles. (Just think: all the television meteorologists would be out of work!) We are able to live with some confidence in a fragile world because we have some assurance that gravity will cause things to drop, rain will cause things to get wet, and the sun will come up again tomorrow. A providential God will not repeal the law of gravity, will not make rain arid, and will not slip a gear on the spinning globe to delay tomorrow's sun. The biblical journey would convince us that God *could* do just that; however, the biblical revelation also is that God reminds God's very self of the covenant God makes with earth. The rainbow is that reminder. The bow is not a sign to us of God's promise; it is God's sign to God—"I will remember my covenant that is between me and you and every living creature of all flesh" (Genesis 9:15a). If God promises not to destroy "all flesh" with the waters of a flood, does that just mean that God will choose other weapons in God's weather arsenal? The prophet Isaiah did not think so.

Isaiah shared the fullness of God's promise:

This is like the days of Noah to me:
  Just as I swore that the waters of Noah
  would never again go over the earth,
so I have sworn that I will not be angry with you
  and will not rebuke you.
For the mountains may depart
  and the hills be removed,
but my steadfast love shall not depart from you,
  and my covenant of peace shall not be removed,
  says the LORD, who has compassion on you.
                                              (Isaiah 54:9-10)

Can the God of all creation change the direction of that creation? God risked just that when God gave humankind "dominion over" (responsibility for) the animals (Genesis 1:26). Human sin has broken the harmony of creation (Genesis 3:15, for example). God's intended created order has been the victim of human sin. The apostle Paul acknowledged that "the creation was subjected to futility, not of its own will but by the will of the one who subjected it" (Romans 8:20). Paul goes on to depict this broken creation as being in bondage to decay (Romans 8:21). If the created order is in bondage to decay, is it any wonder that hurricanes and tornados and earthquakes run out of control? Capricious and damaging natural disasters appear out of the brokenness of creation, the harvest of our sin. Some argue that catastrophe can emerge from global warming, largely the result of human insensitivity to environmental concerns. (Other persons think global warming is part of a natural cycle.) Any way you slice it, there is a connecting point between humankind's sinful break with God and the broken things of creation.

If a storm is about to hit a major city and suddenly shifts and misses that population, has God controlled that change? If a tornado misses a schoolhouse and instead rips up an uninhabited barn, is that God at work? If a flood wipes out the street next to mine and leaves mine un-scathed, is that God's will? For right now, I don't think so, but when we all get to heaven, let's check that out!

If a storm is about to miss a major city and suddenly shifts and blasts that population, has God controlled that change? If a tornado misses an empty barn and tears into an occupied school building, is that God at work? If a flood sweeps away the street where I live and stops short of the next street, is that God's will? For right now, I don't think so, but when we all get to heaven, let's check that out!

Does the mystery of God's hands-on–hands-off relation-ship with natural disasters make God irrelevant in the dis-cussion? No! Even when one claims that God does not act erratically with the forces of nature (the forces of the cre-ated order), one does not claim that God could not if God chose to! Isaiah has captured the nature of this unknown when he speaks of the Creator:

> For my thoughts are not your thoughts,
>   nor are your ways my ways, says the LORD.
> For as the heavens are higher than the earth,
>   so are my ways higher than your ways
>   and my thoughts than your thoughts. (Isaiah 55:8-9)

My region of the country has experienced what weather analysts call "an exceptional drought." Have I joined people of faith throughout our area to pray for rain? Yes. To do so is to acknowledge that God is the Source of all goodness in creation. To do so is to acknowledge our dependence on God's providence. To do so is to acknowledge that a loving God gets thirsty with us when it is dry.

Jesus Christ is the full revelation of God: "And the Word became flesh and lived among us, and we have seen his glory, the glory as of a father's only son, full of grace and truth.... No one has ever seen God. It is God the only Son, who is close to the Father's heart, who has made him known" (John 1:14, 18).

What do we learn about God and "acts of God" when we look at Jesus? Jesus gets angry at things that keep people from God (Luke 19:46). Jesus forgives sin (John 8:11). Jesus is stronger than death (1 Peter 1:3). The acts of God seen in Jesus Christ are acts of love, service, and grace. The acts of God seen in Jesus Christ always point to new life. The acts of God seen in Jesus Christ are mystery beyond our deserving and beyond our understanding. Maybe that's the way it is with acts of God.

SOMETHING TO SAY

Great game, huh? But to get to your question: God gets blamed for a lot of things that are not God's fault. Some people say that God created the races so that some are better than others; that view is human racism. Our sin has brought a lot of pain into our lives. Because of our sin, all of creation is broken down and I suspect that includes some of the power of nature. I wouldn't go so far as to say that God does not have the power to do as God pleases, but Jesus did not see that power as something to be grasped (Philippians 2:6). A flood looks like something God intended for good turning into something bad. Does God permit things God does not will? That's the start of my thinking—sort of a major course in theology in one minute. What do you think?

AFTERWORD

Unless you are the sort who starts reading a book from the back (to find out "whodunit?"), you have probably finished *Ten Questions Every Pastor Fears*. Although I have missed your personal touch, we have studied together, laughed together, and—who knows?—perhaps together even grown spiritually.

It's that "together" part that is important to me. How else can it be for those of us who have been called to a community of faith by a God who is ever forming a people? It is not easy to be together when I am sitting at a computer about five miles from the Bahama, North Carolina, post office and you are at a coffee shop in Boston, or on the back deck of your parsonage in Anchorage, Alaska (how cold is it?), or in your study in Tupelo, Mississippi.

But we can be in this together if both of us agree that struggling with dreaded questions is part of the call God has put upon our lives. But we can be in this together if both of us are willing to be open to being led by the Shepherd into new pastures. But we can be in this together if each of us will acknowledge that the other exists—not only exists but is a stumbling child of God, a God who asks us a question:

"Will you follow me?"
I want to be in this together. Deal?

LET'S KEEP ON TALKING

1. If God is omnipotent (all-powerful), why does God allow things to happen that are not God's will?

2. How is God's love present for those who are afflicted by a natural disaster?

3. What is the relationship among human sin, the environment, and the will of God?

PRAYER

O divine Creator, Source of all that is good, we stumble in the presence of the mysteries of life. You made us to be in harmony with all you created, but we have broken the bonds. You made us to be stewards of your creation, but we have tried to be owners rather than caregivers. Bring your resurrection power for new life. Grant us grace sufficient to live with joy in the midst of ambiguity. Watch over us in the spirit of the one in whose name we pray, even Jesus Christ our Lord. Amen.